REMEMBERING GOUZENKO

The Struggle to Honour a Cold War Hero

Andrew Kavchak

This work is dedicated to the memories of my heroes:
Igor and Svetlana Gouzenko,
and my grandfather Stanisław Kawczak.

CONTENTS

INTRODUCTION TO THE 2019 EDITION

On the day in 2003 that the City of Ottawa unveiled a plaque honouring Igor Gouzenko, the *Ottawa Citizen* published an editorial titled "Remember Gouzenko". It prompted me to call the editors to thank them for the kind words they wrote. The editor I spoke with suggested that I should write a book about this experience of lobbying two levels of government to commemorate Igor Gouzenko with historic plaques. He inspired me. I had kept all my emails, letters and notes of conversations from the four years of agitation in binders. There were eighteen of them. I summarized the contents which I sent to the Mackenzie Institute in Toronto for their consideration. In April 2004 the Mackenzie Institute published the first edition of this text. Copies were sent to Institute members and supporters as well as libraries across Canada. I donated a number of copies to the Ottawa Public Library and the Canadian War Museum.

Over the years I have delivered a number of presentations about Gouzenko to groups of all ages, ranging from students to veterans. I am often asked about the text and where can it be acquired. This updated second edition is long overdue.

This second edition includes some new portions, as well as a few revisions and updates. I thank Evelyn Wilson for her contribution and kind words in her "Appreciation". I hope you enjoy the story.

Andrew Kavchak
October 2019.

FOREWORD BY JOHN C. THOMPSON

Occasionally at the airports of capital cities around the World, a strange procession can be seen: two or three Russian men under heavy escort are whisked from a newly arriving Aeroflot plane directly to their embassy, where they will be confined until it is time to escort them back to the airport and bring in their replacements. Thus, nearly sixty years after Igor Gouzenko's defection, do the Russians rotate the cipher clerks at their embassies around the world.

Gouzenko has a greater legacy than this, and one that deserves what posthumous honours we can pay him. The Soviets were – eventually – our wartime allies against the Axis and they did pay an enormous price for Stalin's temporary trust of Hitler. However, they were an ideological opponent of the Western democracies too and made full use of every safe opportunity to abuse our trust during those days.

Even before Hitler fell, the Soviets violated their agreements with the West and laced our societies with spies. Their apologists and fifth columnists in Western Communist Parties did whatever they could to ensure we viewed their activities in a favorable light and took no action against them. Igor Gouzenko changed all that.

3

It is hard to imagine his defection in 1945, a frightened man and wife, frantically scuttling about Ottawa, trying to get someone to pay attention to their claims, before his superiors at the Soviet embassy noticed that their cipher clerk and over a hundred vital documents were missing. He had reason to be terrified – the very least he might have received if caught would have been a bullet in his brain and those of his pregnant wife and child, and there were much crueler fates available from the Soviet Union.

Fortunately, eventually, we did pay attention – and the rest is history. But we are a country that pays too little attention to our history. After the spy rings were broken and the new defensive alliances were formed to stem the Soviets, Gouzenko became a neglected figure, save that eventually he became a figure of fun. He was derided (especially by the left) for his rare appearances in a hood, and a seemingly paranoid lifestyle. Few Canadians realized that, once the Cold War was over and we were able to read all the records of its main intelligence agency, the Soviets really did want to kill him if they could find him. They were still looking for him in the 1980s.

Andrew Kavchak's account of Gouzenko is a simple reminder of a Canadian hero. The account of his Kafkaesque ordeal to erect a simple plaque to the memory of Gouzenko's historic defection from Soviet service is somewhat more disturbing. Governments never do anything simply and complexity is exponential – having to work with two levels of government is four times as much work; the more so if neither cares to remember what should not have been forgotten.

John C. Thompson
President of the Mackenzie Institute
March, 2004.

PREFACE BY ALEXANDRIA BOIRE

cold war, *n. 1. Intense political, military, and ideological rivalry between nations, short of armed conflict, 2. (caps.) Such rivalry after World War II between the U.S.S.R. and the U.S. and their respective allies.*

WEBSTER'S DICTIONARY

The Cold War. My father, Igor Gouzenko, was said to have started it. Unfortunately, he was the man who was better known in Canada for wearing a white "bag" over his head when being interviewed, than for changing the course of history. In actual fact he was a brave, young man and he warned the West of terrible things in their midst.

Andrew Kavchak has written a book which provides an account of an *"ordinary tax paying Canadian citizen's"* struggle to honour an important historical event. He dedicates the book in part to my parents, whom he refers to as "*my heroes*".

Notwithstanding the tremendous pleasure and honour it gives me, the second daughter of Igor and Svetlana, to write this preface for Andrew's book, I would like to explain how difficult it has been to adjust to first hearing in public, then seeing in print such a deserving acknowledgement of my parents' courage. Andrew's "*heroes*" have been my heroes also, but there has never been a forum for me to publicly exalt that sentiment.

Until now.

Calumny was the fabric of daily life and defending ourselves against this political force was the norm. We were Canadian citizens. We lived under an assumed name, the intent of the new identity being to protect us from political and Soviet reprisals from within Canada and abroad. Anxiety and conflict were the backdrop of life lived in tandem with an "ordinary" life of school, piano lessons and playing tag with childhood friends on summer evenings. I was surrounded by my siblings and the love of my parents and their creative natures, but caution was ubiquitous.

Few incidents in life withstood the scrutiny of my parents' probing minds. Everything was questions, and as a child, my confusion grew. They had done a brave thing for Canada, risked their lives and even sacrificed my knowing my grandparents, and yet, I was not to talk about it to anyone. It must remain a secret. In this difficult and contradictory atmosphere, we children grew up, expanded our horizons, prospered as individuals and went out to find lives for ourselves. For the most part we were successful, but always perplexed, often disappointed and dare I say, frequently angry. The subject of Gouzenko in the media was seldom benign.

It seemed to me that, despite the praise for my father's character and his courageous deeds as reported in the Royal Commission into the Gouzenko Affair in 1946, their positive remarks were overshadowed by the denigrations of those interested in rewriting history. Except for a few conscientious individuals (journalists, politicians, legal experts) whom my father met and learned to trust, there were many years of isolation.

Then Andrew Kavchak entered our life. Someone had contacted us who wanted to publicly honour the historic event and heroism of Igor and Svetlana Gouzenko!

When I learned of this from my sister, Evy, I have to confess that my initial reaction was disbelief and doubt. Who was this person and what were his motives? It was a rare occurrence that someone outside our family could share our convictions and be committed to openly pursuing a cause. Andrew's intelligent, historically informed, persistent nature changed that experience for me. His desire was to recognize, by a government plaque placed in a public park, a critical turning point in Canada's history. Gouzenko's brave actions documented the proof that Stalin had successfully penetrated high levels of government in western democracies. This information created serious fall-out in the free world. I knew it would take a miracle for someone to manoeuver through those politically charged waters, to survive and to succeed. It is because of this success that in my correspondence with Andrew I include the initials W.O.M. after his name. They stand for "worker of miracles".

However, Andrew gives the impression that he was not expecting the extent of bureaucratic delays in the process of getting the plaque erected. Interestingly, there are no references or conjectures in this book to the obstacles being *Political* in nature. I, on the other hand, would tend to overstate and simply contend, it's *only 'political.'*

Each page of this book describes Andrew Kavchak's tenacity. It takes that quality to keep the faith when all seems lost. Victory over that which seems too large, too powerful, too overwhelming to even comprehend dinting its armour, let alone overcoming, is sweet when the initiative was based on the essential quality of doing the right thing. Diligence and principled action! I hope it is contagious.

Andrew has brought a breath of fresh air to our family. This energetic young man recounts in this book, a trip fraught with rejection, bureaucratic bungling and political cowardice surrounding issues deemed *sensitive* by our government. Hooray for those who never give up. Hooray for those who take risks for the benefit of democratic freedoms. And hooray for those who believe that it is imperative to remember those who did.

It is heartening to know that among a new generation of Canadians there is an Andrew Kavchak. His character is comforting to me, and when I sing "We stand on guard for thee, O Canada!" I know it to be true.

Alexandria Boire
December, 2003.

INTRODUCTION

This book contains several intertwined stories. First, this is a book about a young twenty-six year old man who, in an act of uncommon courage, and at great personal risk and a subsequent lifetime of sacrifice, changed the course of history. This is also a story about the project I pursued to commemorate and honour my hero, Igor Gouzenko, in a manner that I felt was long overdue. Further, it is a story about increasing the public's awareness of some amazing things that have happened in our country that shaped world history.

This is also a story about a family which had a heavy, but necessary, veil of security partially lifted to reveal their personal identities. A family, which has been the subject of countless attempts to unfairly discredit their father, was given the pride of knowing that the people of Canada acknowledge and appreciate the great lasting contribution that their parents made to our freedom, and taken measures to show the respect that is so deserved.

In spite of the West's victory in the Cold War and the disintegration of the Soviet Empire, the quest to commemorate Igor Gouzenko brought initial resistance similar to that experience by Gouzenko in 1945. Although the ending is positive, it did not come easily. Anyone who finds bureaucratic bungling a source of amusement will enjoy this tale. Those who lament the lack of efficiency and the excess of waste will find confirmation of their beliefs. This is a story about red tape, delays, bureaucratic timidity and the application of Murphy's Law (everything that can go wrong, will go wrong). As James H. Boren would say, this book illustrates the bureaucratic behavioural principles of "dynamic inaction", "constructive non-responsiveness" and its unwavering commitment to the preservation of the *status quo.*[1]

This story is a case study of how government bureaucracies deal with perceived sensitive files and reveals some of the characteristics of civil service bureaucracies and their inhabitants. It should be of interest to students of political science, public administration, history, sociology, and psychology. This is also a story about pursuing a dream, overcoming adversity and resistance, and not giving up. One must persevere to be successful. It makes the prize at the end all the more sweet and meaningful.

The story is generally conveyed in a chronological order of events. Pursuant to my legal background and experience I kept a file of my correspondence and took detailed notes of each telephone conversation. I had no idea when this project started that the file would eventually occupy several shelves. The correspondence I received from the Minister of Heritage and the Mayor of Ottawa were on official stationary and letterheads of their respective offices. The rest of the correspondence includes exchanges between an individual taxpaying citizen and civil servant employees in the federal and municipal government bureaucracies. None of the correspondence was marked confidential or privileged and none contained any conditions or warnings regarding public disclosure. Headings are used to make it easier for the reader to follow the story. Typographical errors, misused capital letters and misspellings in correspondence have been

---

[1] James H. Boren, *When in Doubt, Mumble – A Bureaucrat's Handbook.* Toronto: Van Nostrand Reinhold Company, 1972.

corrected. Similarly, any irrelevant or personal content of email messages was omitted.

There are many people to thank for their assistance in making my dream of commemorating a hero become reality and making this story eventful enough to commit to paper. First, I wish to thank Igor and Svetlana Gouzenko. Their courage, and the inspiration it provided, is what this book is all about. They are true heroes to whom we probably owe more than we will ever know. I also wish to thank Evelyn Wilson, eldest daughter and spokesperson for the Gouzenko family, as well as her sister Alexandria Boire. Their support and appreciation for the project, from the moment we connected, have meant a great deal to me.

There are many people at the City of Ottawa who have been involved during the four years that I pursued this project. I would like to thank all the politicians and staff who helped more it along, especially former Mayor Jim Watson, Councillor Elisabeth Arnold and Mayor Bob Chiarelli. Mayor Watson's early indication that the city of Ottawa would unveil a plaque was a point of no return which inspired me to persevere when the obstacles seemed insurmountable.

At the federal level I would like to express my gratitude to Heritage Minister Sheila Copps. Her historic designation of the "Gouzenko Affair (1945-1946)" proved to be a major turning point for this project. I would also like to thank all the members and staff at the Historic Sites and Monuments Board of Canada (HSMBC) who helped move this project forward, especially Michael Audy and John Grenville.

There are a number of journalists who did a superb job of conveying the story to the public. Again, I have to thank Jim Watson, this time in his capacity as a municipal affairs columnist for the *Ottawa Citizen* and host on the New RO television station in Ottawa. I would also like to thank Jeff

Sallot, Joy Malbon, Alison Smith, Steve Fisher, Brent Bambury, Bernard St-Laurent, Adam Grachnik, Karen Solomon, Karen Murray, Alex Munter, and Holly Lake. Special words of thanks go to Patrick Dare, Editor of the Editorial Page at the Citizen, for encouraging me to write this book.

Also, I wish to thank The Mackenzie Institute for their willingness to publish this story, as well as Branka Lapajne, Ph.D., for her inimitable editing skills.

Finally, I wish to thank my wife Sylvie for her loving patience and support, and my father, Andrew Kawczak, for having taught me how to assess the failed communist experiment and appreciate the freedoms of liberal democracy.

Andrew Kavchak
Ottawa, March 2004.

CHAPTER 1: THE FLIGHT TO FREEDOM

Igor Gouzenko

Igor Sergeievich Gouzenko was born in 1919 in the village of Rogachov, not far from Moscow.[2] He was the youngest of four children. His father died of typhus in 1919. The third child, a boy born in 1917, died of malnutrition after one year. His remaining siblings were a sister, Ira, and a brother, Vselvolod. His mother was a teacher. Igor attended primary and secondary schools and later entered the Academy of Engineering in Moscow. After only two months, he was sent to a special school conducted under the aegis of the General Staff of the Red Army. It was at his school that he learned the secret codes he would later employ. Gouzenko was then sent to the Main Intelligence Division of the Red Army in Moscow. During that year he saw, in the course of his work, a large number of telegrams to and from many countries, detailing operations similar to those which he was subsequently to encounter in Canada. In late 1942, Soviet authorities decided to send Gouzenko abroad. After a thorough investigation by the NKVD he was sent to Canada.

---

[2] The information in this chapter is based on the following sources: Igor Gouzenko, *This was my Choice*. Toronto: J.M. Dent & Sons (Canada) Limited, 1948).; Canada, 1946. Royal Commission to Investigate the Disclosure of Secret and Confidential Information to Unauthorized Persons (Final Report); and Robert Bothwell and J.L. Granatstein, (eds.). *The Gouzenko Transcripts*. Ottawa: Deneau Publishers & Company Ltd., 1982.

Gouzenko's Arrival in Canada

On August 23, 1939, the Nazis and the Soviets signed a non-aggression pact which was meant to ensure peace between the two regimes. However, the pact was accompanied by secret protocols which delineated their respective spheres of influence, and divided Poland between them. This was the green light for the start of World War II and six years of merciless aggression.[3]

On September 1, 1939, Hitler attacked Poland and proceeded to occupy the Western half of the country. Great Britain and France declared war on Germany on September 3. On September 10 Canada did the same. However, on September 17 the Soviet Union attacked Poland from the East and proceeded to occupy its half of Poland as previously agreed with Nazi Germany. No one declared war on the Soviet Union. The Soviets then went to war with Finland and took measures to assert control over Lithuania, Latvia and Estonia, as well as Bessarabia. During the period between 1939 and 1941, the two totalitarian regimes significantly assisted each other in their war efforts through increased trade. Canada did not have formal diplomatic relations with the Soviet Union and the Nazi-Soviet Pact did not help. The Communist Party of Canada agitated against the war effort and was banned. However, Hitler's decision to invade the Soviet Union in June 1941 dramatically altered the situation. The Soviet Union then joined the common struggle to defeat Nazi Germany. At the end of 1942 Canada and the U.S.S.R. announced that they would exchange diplomatic missions. The Soviets established their mission in an old mansion in Ottawa in an area known as Sandy Hill. The Communist Party reconstituted itself as the Labour Progressive Party and ran candidates in elections across Canada.

---

[3] The Protocols became known when the Nazi regime's documents were captured by Western forces at the end of the war.

Gouzenko arrived in Canada in June 1943 via Siberia, Alaska and Western Canada. He arrived in Edmonton by air, completing the rest of the journey by train. His wife, Svetlana, joined him in October, 1943, and soon there son Andrei was born. Gouzenko's official title was that of "civilian employee" of the Soviet Embassy in Ottawa, although he held the rank of Lieutenant in the Red Army. Gouzenko worked as a cipher clerk under the military attaché, Colonel Zabotin. In fact, Gouzenko and Zabotin both worked for Soviet military intelligence (GRU). In his work of coding and decoding messages between the Embassy and Moscow, Gouzenko became aware of a spy network which had penetrated the Canadian government, as well as those of the U.S. and Britain.

After only a short time in Canada, the Gouzenkos realized that the propaganda they had been fed in the Soviet Union about life in the West did not correspond to reality. The Gouzenkos were impressed with freedom in Canada, particularly during the elections. They were also impressed with the abundance of goods for sale in the stores, including food that could be purchased by anybody, and not just government officials or party members.

The End of World War II

Hitler committed suicide on April 30, 1945, after receiving reports that Soviet tanks had penetrated Berlin and were approaching his bunker. The German unconditional surrender was signed at Eisenhower's headquarters at Reims on May 7, 1945. After the surrender the fighting in Europe ceased. The allies had previously agreed to divide Germany into four occupation zones. The respective military commanders exercised administrative authority, but almost immediately tension and difficulties developed between the Soviets and the Western powers.

When the Western leaders met with Stalin at Yalta in February, 1945, they had agreed that all countries freed from German occupation would be permitted representative governments through free and unfettered elections. Unfortunately, the Soviets started violating this agreement from the moment it was signed. In the countries the Soviets took over they imposed their communist puppets as rulers, and used brutal force and terror to paralyze any resistance.

In early August, 1945 the Americans dropped two atomic bombs on the Japanese cities of Hiroshima and Nagasaki. On September 2, 1945, in a ceremony aboard the deck of the *USS Missouri* in Tokyo Bay, the Japanese formally surrendered, ending World War II. Years of worldwide bloodshed came to an end and peace was finally a possibility.

However, the world war was followed by an era that came to be known as the "Cold War". It was marked by a rapid deterioration in relations and escalating tension between the U.S.S.R. and the Western countries. A series of crises would mark the decades that followed. One such incident, often considered the very first to put the Soviet Union at odds with its former allies, occurred just three days after the Japanese surrender. The incident did not occur in Berlin, London, or Washington, but in Canada's capital, Ottawa.

In late 1944, Moscow sent a telegram to Zabotin indicating that Gouzenko was required to return to the Soviet Union. Zabotin made sufficient representations to allow Gouzenko to remain a while longer. However, in August, 1945, Moscow ordered that Gouzenko must return with his wife and child. When Gouzenko was informed that he was due to return to Moscow, he discussed the situation with his twenty-two year old wife, now pregnant with their second child. They decided on a daring plan. Gouzenko believed that the West needed to be warned of the threat posed by Stalin.

They were fully aware of the danger and risks that their decision involved. In 1937 a Soviet spy in Western Europe, Ignace Reiss, wrote a letter to Stalin in which he declared his withdrawal from the Soviet apparatus. A month later he was assassinated in Switzerland. In 1940 exiled Soviet revolutionary Leon Trotsky was assassinated in Mexico. Similarly, Walter Krivitsky, a former Soviet spy in Western Europe who defected before the war and predicted the Nazi-Soviet Pact, was found dead in a Washington hotel room in 1941. Clearly, the Soviets were capable of going to great lengths and distances to exact revenge.

Wednesday, September 5, 1945

On Wednesday, September 5, 1945, Gouzenko walked out of the Soviet Embassy with 109 documents, consisting of evidence of Soviet espionage, stuffed under his shirt. Getting out of the Embassy about 8 p.m., without arousing suspicion and avoiding an unexpected invitation to join his colleagues for a movie, was his first challenge, but by no means the hardest.

Gouzenko had never considered going to the police. Based on his experience with the NKVD, he suspected there might be a Soviet spy in their midst. Instead, he took a streetcar to the *Ottawa Journal* newspaper offices. He approached the *Journal* because he had been impressed with the freedom and the fearlessness of the Canadian press. By going to the press, he hoped that if the newspaper broke the story and published his reasons for breaking with the Soviet Union, the Canadian authorities would take him in. If he were to be subsequently murdered by the Soviet secret police, the information would be public and spark an even greater interest in Soviet activities.

He entered the building, but suddenly had doubts about whether this was the right place to go to. It was conceivable that an NKVD agent was working at the newspaper. Then a young lady recognized him and asked what he was doing there and whether there was any news breaking at the Embassy. He quickly dodged the question by apologizing that he was in a hurry. He returned to his apartment to speak with his wife, who gave him renewed confidence. He returned to the *Journal*, only to be told that the editor had left for the night. He walked to the nearest desk in the City Room where he explained who he was and that he had documents proving Soviet agents in Canada were seeking data on the atomic bomb. The journalist, who had just been given the scoop of the century, told Gouzenko that he was busy and suggested he either go to the RCMP or come back in the morning to see the editor. A plea that the NKVD might be on his trail and try to kill him, did not change the journalist's mind.

Gouzenko then walked to the Department of Justice building on Wellington Street, hoping to see the Minister of Justice. Unfortunately, an RCMP officer replied that it was too late and he could not see anybody until the morning. A subsequent plea generated no change in response. Gouzenko returned to his apartment in a state of fear. His wife tried to bolster his spirits, but they both had difficulty sleeping.

Thursday, September 6, 1945

In the morning Gouzenko, his wife and their two year old son, went to the Justice building. They had decided to place the documents in Svetlana's purse, convinced that if the NKVD found the Gouzenkos the first person they would go after would be Igor. At the Justice building he explained that he had to see the Minister on a matter of absolute urgency. He was escorted to the Minister's office, where he explained to the secretary that the matter was such that he could only speak to the Minister about it. He was then escorted from the Justice building to the Minister's office on Parliament Hill, where the Minister was. After going through the same discussion with another secretary, they were escorted back to the Justice building and told to wait there. They waited for two hours, before being informed that the Minister was unable to see them.

Igor was about to panic, but Svetlana quietly suggested they go back to the newspaper office. At the *Ottawa Journal*, they were told that the editor was unavailable. However, they did explain their story to a journalist who went to the editor's office. When the reporter returned, he said that nobody wanted to say anything but nice things about Stalin. The reporter suggested they go to the RCMP to inquire about taking out naturalization papers. By this time, the Gouzenkos were desperate and returned to the Justice building. An officer there informed them that the RCMP had nothing to do with naturalization and told them to go to the Crown Attorney's office on Nicholas Street.

At the Crown Attorney's office they were told that the lady who handled naturalization applications was at lunch. Going for lunch themselves, Igor noted the time as being 1:45 p.m. and felt that by now the embassy staff had probably noticed the missing documents and were wondering why he had not shown up for work. When their son Andrei fell asleep at the lunch table, they decided to take him back to their Somerset Street apartment and ask a neighbor, in the next building, to babysit him. They explained to the neighbor that they wanted to do some shopping before returning to Moscow. Then they returned to the Crown Attorney's office, only to be told that the naturalization process could take several months. Upon hearing this, Svetlana's courage failed her and she burst into tears. Another lady, who had spoken to the Gouzenkos earlier, was in sight and Igor quickly approached and told her their story. She listened in amazement, and then brought a couple of chairs over to the desk so the Gouzenkos could be seated. "This is something the world should know. I will try to help you." was her response. Unfortunately, a call to another newspaper reporter elicited the familiar lack of interest.

Unsuccessful in their quest, the Gouzenkos decided to return home. Igor carefully entered his apartment first. Satisfied that all was clear, he waved to his wife who had picked up their son in the neighbouring building, indicating that they could come home. They were exhausted and in need of rest and time to think and plan their next move. A short time later Gouzenko looked out of the front window of their second story apartment and his heart nearly stopped. Two men were seated on a bench in Dundonald Park, directly opposite, and both were looking up at his window! He did not recognize them, but stepped back from the curtain so that his shadow could not be seen. He noticed that they alternatively chatted and looked up at his window. Suddenly, a knock sounded on the apartment door. Igor and Svetlana remained quiet. There was a second louder, more insistent knock, which was repeated four times. Suddenly their son dashed across the floor and then a fist banged on the door and a voice called out "Gouzenko!" Igor recognized the voice as Under-Lieutenant Lavrentiev, Zabotin's chauffeur. Lavrentiev called out Gouzenko's name several times before departing.

A crucial moment had arrived. If they stayed put they were doomed and they knew it. It was 7:05 p.m. Igor decided to go to his rear balcony and attempt to make contact with a neighbour, Sergeant Harold Main of the Royal Canadian Air Force, who was on his rear balcony. Gouzenko quickly got to the point. He and his wife expected the NKVD to make an attempt on their lives and they were worried about their son. Sergeant Main was doubtful, but after Igor brought his attention to the presence of the two men on the park bench, he changed his opinion. When they noticed a man walking in the laneway at the back of the apartment building, looking up, Sergeant Main told Gouzenko to get his wife and son over to his apartment and he would get the police. By this point Gouzenko was no longer alarmed by the thought of contacting the police. When Gouzenko returned to his apartment he saw his wife, with their son, talking to the neighbour from the apartment directly across the hall, Mrs. Francis Elliott. Upon hearing the story, Mrs. Elliot suggested they stay with her for the night. Her husband and son were away and there was a day bed they could use. The Gouzenkos gratefully accepted. Sergeant Main then set off on his bicycle to seek police assistance.

Soon after there were heavy footsteps in the hall. Sergeant Main had returned with two Ottawa constables. Gouzenko recounted the story and expressed their fears of being killed. The constables, Thomas Walsh and John McCulloch, asked some questions and then spoke with Mrs. Elliott. The constables said that they would keep the building under observation all night. They suggested leaving the light in the bathroom on all night, as it showed on Somerset Street. If something happened, the signal would be to turn off the light and the police would come up. The Gouzenkos were relieved and the constables left.

Around 10 p.m. Gouzenko pulled up the window blind. There was nobody below. Then, the drama intensified. Between 11:30 p.m. and midnight Igor and his wife suddenly awoke to the sound of knocking on their apartment door, across the hallway. Gouzenko looked through the keyhole and could see clearly Pavlov, the Second Secretary of the Embassy and head of the NKVD in Canada, knocking on their door. With him were three thugs from the Embassy, Lieutenant-Colonel Rogov, Military Attaché, Soviet Air Force; Lieutenant Angelov, Member of the staff of the Military Attaché; and Pavlov's cipher clerk, Alexander Farafontov. At this point Sergeant Main opened his door and asked the men what they wanted. When they indicated they were looking for Gouzenko, the Sergeant replied that the Gouzenkos were away. Pavlov thanked him and the four went downstairs, as though to leave. Instead, they returned quietly. Gouzenko looked through the keyhole to see Pavlov working on the door to their apartment with a jimmy. There was a rasping sound and the door opened. The four NKVD men entered and closed the door behind them. Mrs. Elliott then told Gouzenko that she had turned the light on and off, but the police were not coming. She asked him what she should do. Igor told her to call the police on the telephone. She called and told them that someone was trying to break into apartment 4, 511 Somerset Street.

Shortly afterward the same two constables appeared at the apartment door. Constable Walsh did not wait for any formality but threw open the door. Together with Constable McCulloch they caught the four men in the act of riffling through Gouzenko's desk and bureau drawers. The Gouzenkos opened the door to Mrs. Elliott's apartment a crack, so as to be able to listen to what was going on. Constable Walsh asked for an explanation and Pavlov replied that the apartment belonged to a man from the Soviet Embassy who happened to be in Toronto. He had left some documents and they had his permission to look for them. Constable Walsh inquired whether they were also given permission to break the lock. Pavlov did not back down, but insisted that they lost the key to the apartment. Besides, he stated, the lock was Soviet property and they could do what they wanted with it. Pavlov then ordered the two constables to leave the apartment. Constable Walsh looked at his colleague, and then said they would remain until the Inspector arrived to check their identification.

Inspector Macdonald finally came and asked more extensive questions, which upset Pavlov. He claimed that the constables had insulted them and that their Soviet diplomatic immunity had been assailed. The Inspector told them to wait while he left to make some inquiries. However, after he was gone Pavlov told the other three to leave with him. The two Ottawa constables made no effort to stop them.

Friday, September 7, 1945

In the morning another Ottawa city police inspector came and knocked on the door of the apartment where the Gouzenkos were staying. He told them that the RCMP would like to have a talk with Gouzenko at the Justice Building. Finally, someone was listening. Igor went to the Justice Building where high-ranking RCMP and civilian investigators were waiting. For five hours they discussed his documents and asked questions. Gouzenko requested to be kept in protective custody, as he feared for his safety and that of his family.

When he described his difficulties in getting someone to listen to him, the RCMP officer in charge replied that he had not been neglected after all, that he and his partner had sat on the park bench watching the apartment. It turned out that, during the two hours the Gouzenkos had waited outside the Justice Minister's office, the Department of External Affairs and the RCMP had been pondering over what to do. Prime Minister MacKenzie King had been consulted, and was primarily concerned with the potential damage this could cause in his relations with Stalin. However, his assistants convinced him that returning Gouzenko and his documents to the Soviet Embassy might not be the wisest course of action. It had been decided to "shadow" Gouzenko to see what happened and determine if he was who he claimed to be. Ironically, it was Pavlov's breaking into Gouzenko's apartment which convinced Canadian authorities that Gouzenko had a real story to tell.

The Gouzenkos were subsequently taken to a secret military camp near Whitby, on Lake Ontario, called Camp X. The family stayed there in a safe house for two years with RCMP protection. Gouzenko concluded his autobiography by saying that in spite of the difficulties, he would do it again, because he felt it was his duty toward the millions of enslaved and voiceless in the Soviet empire.

The Aftermath

On the centenary of the RCMP in 1973 former Deputy Commissioner, William Kelly, wrote a book about its history. The opening sentence to chapter nineteen titled *"Soviet Espionage 1945-1949"*, reads: *"Probably the most important investigation in the history of the Force, and consequently in the history of Canada, began in Ottawa on September 7, 1945."*[4] Although the RCMP had known for some years that the Soviet Embassy was recruiting agents, Kelly states, *"...the documents Gouzenko had removed from the*

---

[4] Nora and William Kelly, *The Royal Canadian Mounted Police*. Edmonton: Hurtig Publishers, 1973, p. 203.

Embassy files and turned over to the police disclosed an espionage network far more insidious than the police had suspected."[5]

In the period immediately following the defection the RCMP attempted to gather as much evidence as possible relating to Gouzenko's revelations. The Government kept the whole matter secret, although Prime Minister Mackenzie King travelled to Washington and London to personally inform President Truman and Prime Minister Attlee of what had transpired and to discuss further cooperation.

The American news media broke the story in early February 1946 and the Gouzenko Affair then came to light in Canada. At this point Mackenzie King was on the hot seat with respect to what had happened and what the government was going to do about it. Unable to conceal it any longer, on February 5, 1946, the government appointed a Royal Commission of Inquiry. Led by two Justices of the Supreme Court of Canada, the mandate was to "investigate the facts relating to and the circumstances surrounding the communication, by public officials and other persons in positions of trust of secret and confidential information to agents of a foreign power."

The 1946 Taschereau-Kellock Royal Commission

After reviewing the available evidence for one week, on February 14, the Commission recommended the arrest of certain individuals. The following day thirteen suspects were arrested. The Commission heard Gouzenko's testimony and examined all the evidence available to it. The Royal Commission's final Report was dated June 27, 1946, and made public on July 15, 1946. The Report concluded by stating:

---

[5] Kelly, ibid, p. 203.

"Having heard that evidence [Gouzenko's] and the evidence of other witnesses who came into contact with Gouzenko on September 6th and 7th, 1945, we have been impressed with the sincerity of the man, and with the manner in which he gave his evidence, which we have no hesitation in accepting."[6]

The Report noted that there was one espionage network operated by Zabotin (GRU). However, there were also parallel military networks, a political network, a naval intelligence network, and an NKVD ring. Information had been secured only about Zabotin's ring, but there was evidence that Zabonin's net was linked to others in the U.S. and Britain.

The Royal Commission Report went on to state the truly memorable phrase:

"In our opinion Gouzenko, by what he has done, has rendered great public service to the people of this country, and thereby has placed Canada in his debt."[7]

The Royal Commission's work was followed with the prosecution of twenty alleged spies. However, the Crown prosecutors encountered numerous legal obstacles which the accused were able to rely on. For example, there were legal difficulties in accepting as evidence stolen embassy materials. The government was not always willing or able, to introduce the evidence that the Royal Commission had secretly received. The accused did not always have immediate access to counsel and if the accused did not make full and voluntary confessions there was little alternative evidence that the prosecutors could use.[8] In the end almost half of the accused walked free.

---

[6] Canada, Ibid, p. 637.

[7] Canada, Ibid, p. 637.

[8] Bothwell and Granatstein, Ibid, p. 14-15.

Those who were convicted included: Fred Rose (Member of Parliament – six years); Sam Carr (six years); Gordon Lunan (five years); Durnford Smith (five years); Harold Gerson (five years); Edward Mazerall (four years); Kathleen Willsher (three years); Emma Woikin (two and a half years); Dr. Raymond Boyer (two years); and John Soboloff ($500 fine and costs).

Those who were acquitted at their initial trial were: Israel Halperin, Frederick Poland, Eric Adams, Matt Nightingale, David Shugar, Agatha Chapman and W.M. Pappin.

Henry Harris and James Benning were acquitted on appeal. Freda Linton's charges were withdrawn.

Also convicted was Alan Nunn May, the first of the atom bomb spies to be caught. He had returned to England after the war and was arrested by British authorities. He was sentenced to ten years, and released after having served six and a half.

The Impact on Soviet Espionage

In the years since the collapse of the Soviet empire much historical information has come out revealing the contents of KGB files. *The Mitrokhin Archive*, an authoritative account of Soviet intelligence activities, revealed that according to a damage report prepared to assess the impact of Gouzenko's defection, his defection had "paralyzed" Soviet intelligence efforts in Canada for years and continued to have a negative effect up to 1960.[9]

---

9 Christopher Andrew and Vasili Mitrokhin, *The Mitrokhin Archive*. Toronto: The Penguin Press, 1999, p. 181.

In addition, in November 1962 a list was drawn up of individuals whom KGB Chairman Semichastny considered "particularly dangerous traitors" and against whom he approved a plan of "special actions" (i.e. assassination). The oldest name on the list was that of Igor Gouzenko.[10]

Gouzenko's Life in Canada

The Gouzenko Affair was a great sensation when it became public. Gouzenko himself was named "Newsmaker of the Year" in 1946. The Gouzenkos were given a new identity and took security pre-cautions for the rest of their lives. In 1948 Gouzenko wrote his autobiography: *This Was My Choice*[11], which was subsequently turned into a 20th Century Fox Hollywood movie titled: *The Iron Curtain*, staring Dana Andrews and Gene Tierney. In 1954, he wrote a novel: *The Fall of a Titan*[12], for which he won the Governor General's literary awarded for fiction. Also, in 1954 another movie was made about the Gouzenko story titled: *Operation Manhunt*, staring Harry Townes and Irje Jensen. In 1960 Svetlana Gouzenko wrote: *Before Igor: Memoirs of My Soviet Youth*.[13]

Gouzenko made several appearances on television shows, but always wore a hood over his head to protect his identify. The hood became his trademark.

Igor and Svetlana Gouzenko paid an enormous price for their courage, including sacrificing their careers and peace of mind. Their families in the U.S.S.R. also suffered the consequences, as Stalin exacted his revenge with the usual punishment of innocents. When subjected to public criticism by

---

[10] Andrew and Mitrokhin, Ibid, p. 477–478.

[11] Gouzenko, *This Was My Choice*, Ibid.

[12] Igor Gouzenko, *The Fall of a Titan*, New York: W.W. Norton & Company, Inc. 1954.

[13] Svetlana Gouzenko, *Before Igor*. London: Cassel & Company Ltd, 1961 (British Edition).

Soviet sympathizers, it appeared that Igor Gouzenko had also sacrificed his reputation and dignity.

In 1997 two historians wrote a Canadian bestseller titled *The Canadian 100 – The 100 Most Influential Canadians of the 20th Century*. Igor Gouzenko was among the one hundred. The authors concluded that without Gouzenko, it would have taken longer for the democracies to wake up to the new threat posed by the Soviet Union.[14]

Igor and Svetlana Gouzenko had a total of eight children. Igor Gouzenko died in June, 1982 and was buried at a secret location in an unmarked grave.

How Igor and Svetlana Gouzenko Became my Heroes

Igor and Svetlana Gouzenko had a close call with the NKVD, and were fortunate enough to survive. I wish I could say the same about my grandfather, but I can't. His fate was different. My paternal Grandfather, Stanisław Kawczak, was a lieutenant in the Polish division of the Austrian army at the beginning of World War I. He survived the war, became a lawyer in Warsaw, married, and had one son, my father. In 1936, he published his memoirs, entitled *Milknace Echa, Wspomnienia z Wojny 1914-1920* (Dying Echoes – Memories of the War 1914-1920). The book was subsequently banned by the Communists and did not reappear in print until 1991, when Poland was once again a free country.

In 1978 Professor Julian Krzyzanowski, a leading authority on Polish literature, wrote that *"best of the memoirs about the war in Europe was S. Kawczak's book of reminiscences* Dying Echoes (Milknace Echa) *of the*

---

[14] H. Graham Rawlinson and J.L. Granatstein, *The Canadian 100*. Toronto: McArther & Company, 1997, p. 199.

[15] Julian Krzyzanowski, *A History of Polish Literature*. Warsaw: Pwn–Polish Scientific Publishers, 1978, p. 648.

heroic deeds of Jerzy Dobodzicki (later a general), who organized the Polish soldiers on the Italian front for their future tasks in the liberated motherland."[15]

As World War II approached, my grandfather was caught up in the general mobilization as an officer (captain) in the Polish army. He was captured by the invading Soviet forces in September 1939 and taken to a camp in the Soviet Union known as Starobelsk. It was one of three such camps where the Soviets kept thousands of Polish officers. In 1943, the Nazis uncovered mass graves in the Katyn forest containing thousands of Polish officers who were murdered in 1940 by the NKVD on Stalin's orders. Those officers had been held at the Kozelsk camp. The mass graves of the Polish officers who held at Starobelsk and Ostashkov were not located until the 1990s. The mass murder of all the Polish officers at the multiple locations became known as the Katyn Forest Massacre. The Nazis were quick to use their discovery at Katyn to disseminate anti-Soviet propaganda relating to this war crime. Although the Nazis were just as good at propaganda as the Soviets, in this case they were telling the truth. The Soviets, however, denied responsibility and claimed that the Nazis had murdered the Polish officers. It was not until Gorbachev's "glasnost" that the Soviets admitted in 1990 they were the ones with blood on their hands. I always regretted that I never had a chance to meet my grandfather and enjoy his company.

My parents managed to leave Poland and settle in Montreal in 1960 where I was born. I visited my relatives in Poland several times in my youth, when it was still a communist country and came to realize how lucky I was to be born in Canada. I eventually studied political science and law and developed an interest in national security issues. In my research on Canadian national security I became familiar with the significant role played by Igor and Svetlana Gouzenko. After what the NKVD had done to my grandfather and millions of other victims of communist oppression, and knowing what their intentions were towards the West, I came to cheer on anyone who gave the

NKVD, and its subsequent incarnation the KGB, a hard time and thwarted them from achieving their objectives. Nobody gave the NKVD a harder time in Canada than Igor Gouzenko. With uncommon courage he did the right thing. That is how Igor Gouzenko became my hero. But he was not alone. His wife Svetlana was the other half of the team.

CHAPTER 2: 1999 – DO SOMETHING!

1989 – First Visit to Dundonald Park

In May, 1989, I moved to an Ottawa suburb after having completed my law degree and my year of articling at a law firm in Toronto. I had moved with the intention of completing the Bar Admission Course in Ottawa and pursuing my career in Canada's capital. One of the first places I visited that summer was Dundonald Park. I sat on a bench across the street from the building at 511 Somerset Street and tried to visualize the events of September 5-7, 1945, in my mind. I looked around. In spite of the drama which had unfolded there and its significance, there was no marker. No plaque. Nothing! I thought that surely somebody must be working on it. Surely it was just a matter of time. Someday there would be a commemorative historic plaque in this location. There had to be.

1999 – On Parental Leave – Let the Lobbying Begin!

Several years later I had married and moved downtown into a townhouse, just three blocks away from Dundonald Park. Following the birth of our first child I went on parental leave in the summer of 1999. During that period I followed a daily routine with my son and we would go to the park where there was a fenced off playground for children. During those visits in July 1999, I looked at the building across the street. There was still no plaque. I began to feel strongly that the erection of a commemorative plaque was long overdue and that the time had come for me to do something. The least I could do was submit a proposal to the appropriate authorities. But who were they?

After each outing my son would usually have a nap. During those windows of opportunity I started to make a few phone calls, send a few emails, and write some letters trying to connect with officials who were in a position to do something. I had written a three page email, which I used with minor variations, to submit proposals to various government officials suggesting a plaque be erected to honour Igor Gouzenko.

In my research I also came across the internet website of the Ministry of the Solicitor General. Since the RCMP Security Service and CSIS owed so much of their existence to Gouzenko, I thought that the relevant Department would be receptive. The website indicated that one could submit a message by email and their service standards included a commitment to respond within a month. Accordingly, I sent them my proposal. I never heard back from them.

I sent my Centretown Ottawa Member of Parliament (M.P.), Mr. Mac Harb, a copy of my standard email. As he was my representative in the federal legislature, and the M.P. for the area where so much of the action took place, I hoped he would be helpful and champion the cause, or at least direct me to the appropriate federal office. I subsequently received an email reply, wherein he dismissed my proposal and suggested that he had "no jurisdiction over the matter". He told me to contact "the city". I contacted his office and left a message stating that there must be a mistake, but it resulted in no change.

I also emailed my local City Councillor Elisabeth Arnold in late July, 1999. One of her assistants called me back and suggested that I apply to the federal Historic Sites and Monuments Board of Canada (HSMBC), which was affiliated with the Department of Canadian Heritage.

Naively, I hoped I could send my proposal to the Minister of Canadian Heritage and that that would be enough to get the ball rolling. On July 28, 1999, I sent an email to the Honourable Sheila Copps, proposing that Heritage Canada unveil a plaque to commemorate Igor Gouzenko. I subsequently received a phone call form one of her assistants suggesting that I should make an application to the HSMBC. This body would then make a recommendation to the Minister regarding a historic designation, which could then be commemorated by means of a plaque. She promised to send me brochures about the Board and how to proceed with my application. A month and a half later I received a letter with the documentation. At the bottom of the letter she had added "Good luck!"

The Historic Sites and Monuments Board of Canada (HSMBC)

The HSMBC was created in 1919 and advises the federal government on sites, events and places of national significance and on appropriate ways of commemorating them. The HSMBC exists pursuant to the authority of the *Historic Sites and Monuments Act*. Its members are appointed by the government. The administrative support for the HSMBC is provided by the Director General of National Historic Sites, Parks Canada. Historians and archaeologists of Parks Canada prepare the necessary historical background material to assist the Board in making its decisions and recommendations on national significance, upon receipt of applications from the public. If the recommendation of the HSMBC is positive and the Minister agrees, the usual form of commemoration is the erection of a bronze plaque at a suitable location, bearing a bilingual inscription. The HSMBC will generally make a positive recommendation to the Minister, regarding a subject for designation, if it satisfies the criteria and the guidelines. The HSMBC receives over 200 applications each year and by 2002 a total of 849 national historic sites, 557 persons and 324 other aspects of Canadian history had received historic designations. Over 1,100 commemorative plaques had been erected across Canada.

I scanned the designation criteria as they applied to persons, places and events. The criteria for a place would be tricky. The criteria are extensive and specific. Yet the Gouzenko drama occurred in several places. It was easy to dispense with the person option, as the criteria required Gouzenko to be deceased for at least 25 years. This was not yet the case. Thus, I determined that the event of Gouzenko's defection and its consequences (The "Gouzenko Affair") would be the most likely to succeed. The criteria for the designation of events were that "an event may be designated of national historic significance if it represents a defining action, episode, movement, or experience in Canadian history." Applicants are required to submit a completed application, including information that identifies the subject in detail and elaborates on the national importance of the subject; existing historical recognition, including the texts of any existing plaques; documentation and references, with cites of historical sources; and suggestions for further research.

As I scanned the materials that had been sent, I started to plan a formal application. It would have to be thorough and well documented in order to avoid being rejected. Drafting an application proved to be a very time-consuming matter. It could potentially involve a great deal of research, for which I did not have sufficient time, as I was about to return to my full-time job. I wondered whether there was another way to stir the HSMBC to action, without my having to spend months writing a thesis.

My Application to the Mayor of the City of Ottawa

On August 4, 1999 I sent an email to the Mayor of Ottawa, Jim Watson, in which I proposed that the City of Ottawa install a commemorative plaque near 511 Somerset Street. In my conclusion I suggest that: *"The cold war is now over and the Western nations prevailed. The Soviet empire has collapsed and the U.S.S.R. no longer exists. As we mark the beginning of the next century and millennium, it is appropriate for us to consider the events of history that occurred in the last century in our own backyard. The events that took place at 511 Somerset Street are significant and deserve to be commemorated by a historical plaque."* I concluded *"...please do not tell me that this is a federal matter. I already communicated this idea to my MP Mac Harb and he said that I should send the idea to the City."*

A few days later, Mayor Watson replied, thanking me for my email and stating: *"I agree that this is a good idea and will look into the possibility with City Staff."*

This was great news. I could not ask for anything more. I had no idea what would happen, but sending a message directly to the Mayor from home obviously got the ball rolling. Although there was no guarantee on what the outcome would be, at least I knew that I had tried.

The Lobbying Efforts Continue

I also wrote to Derek Lee, an MP who was formerly a member of the Thacker Committee which reviewed the CSIS Act in 1989-1990. I suspected he would be familiar with the matter and its significance. Though I received a letter from him in September, stating that it was an interesting suggestion and he would discuss it with some of his Ottawa MP colleagues, I never heard from him again.

Similarly, I had sent my proposal to the leader of the Progressive Conservative Party in the Senate, Senator John Lynch-Staunton. I had personally known the Senator since the late 1970s, as his son Peter was my best friend in high school. In 1990 Prime Minister Brian Mulroney appointed

Mr. Lynch-Staunton to the Senate. Peter's father was obviously better connected than I had ever imagined. In response to my proposal, I received a letter from the Senator in October 1999, enclosing information about the HSMBC. His cover letter stated that the Russians might object, but it was certainly worth a try. He then added the following:

"By the way, my godfather, Raymond Boyer, was one of those named by Gouzenko. He was a chemist who helped develop an explosive more powerful than TNT and passed on the formula to the Soviet Union. He spent some time in jail, and the rest of his life involved in helping to improve jail conditions."

I was grateful to Senator Lynch-Staunton for his package and expression of support.

Another application was sent to Herb Gray, Deputy Prime Minister, who was in charge of the Millennium Bureau of Canada. Millennium celebrations were being planned and the government was inviting applications from Canadians to help celebrate the turn of the century. A letter, in October 1999, from Mr. Gray included the standard celebration application forms, and a note that he had forwarded my proposal to Sheila Copps, Minister of Canadian Heritage. No further communication was forthcoming.

David Kilgour Lends a Hand

My standard proposal email was sent to another MP who I knew had some interest in national security matters. The Honourable David Kilgour, at the time Secretary of State (Latin America and Africa), was thus a Cabinet member. I had read some of his published writings, including one particularly incisive book review which demonstrated a profound understanding of intelligence matters. Some time passed before, on November 1, 1999, an email arrived from his assistant Richard McGuire stating that my original email to David Kilgour has "slipped through the cracks". However, he now asked whether I had made any progress.

I said that I have been referred to the Minister of Canadian Heritage and that I was subsequently referred to the HSMBC. Notwithstanding the fact that they have research historians on staff, it was up to me to fill out a formal application, otherwise the suggestion would go nowhere. I explained that from my perspective the problem was that the guidelines contain and extensive list of criteria and the process was labourious. I had started drafting a submission, but with my newborn son I simply could not find the time. Since I was not related to the Gouzenkos and had no personal interest in this matter, it was disappointing that apparently nothing would happen if I did not submit a complete application. I asked if he could pick up this matter and make a proposal to the HSMBC, or at least provide me with a letter of support.

Following further correspondence we agreed that I would send a proposal to Mr. Kilgour and he would forward it to Heritage Minister Sheila Copps. Accordingly, I sent a letter dated November 10, 1999, to David Kilgour outlining my proposal and the difficulty of getting the HSMBC to move on this subject without my writing a thesis and that I believed the HSMBC should be able to take some initiative of its own. I also copied Mr. Michel Audy, Executive Secretary of the HSMBC, so that this matter would not come as a surprise. I subsequently received a copy of a letter, dated December 29, 1999, from David Kilgour to Sheila Copps enclosing a copy of my letter of November 10, 1999. He told her that I was frustrated by the official response to my suggestion, as I felt the onus should not be on me, as a private individual with limited time, to initiate a complex application to the Board. This was now the third time that Sheila Copps had received one of my letters concerning my Gouzenko plaque proposal.

Year-End Status

My first year of lobbying appeared to end on a positive note. I had managed to get my proposal into the hands of both the Mayor and Heritage Minister. Hopefully, David Kilgour's forwarding my proposal to Sheila Copps would ensure that the HSMBC would start moving on the matter without further action on my part.

During this period I often reflected on the Gouzenko family. I knew that Igor Gouzenko had passed away in 1982, but I did not know if Svetlana was still alive. I had seen her on television in an interview around 1987, but that was it. I wondered what their family was like, where they lived and what they were doing. I wondered whether the children, and grandchildren had an appreciation of what their parents and grandparents had done. I wanted so much to be able to contact them, to tell them about my project so that they could have the satisfaction of knowing that something of this nature was being pursued. Maybe they could even come to the ceremony. I imagined an elderly Svetlana Gouzenko witnessing the unveiling of a commemorative plaque in her and her husband's honour. But there was no point in trying to look for the Gouzenko family. If the Soviets could not find them it was unlikely that I ever could. I figured that if they protected their identity and took protective security measures for so many decades, it was futile for me to even bother starting to look.[16]

---

[16] On February 5, 1989, *The Sunday Star* printed an article by John Picton titled "Gouzenko's wife still makes sure she's not followed". The article revealed that Svetlana Gouzenko put newspapers on the floor in a certain pattern so she'd know if they were disturbed by footprints. Similarly, she continued to jot down suspicious incidents on a pad, to leave a record should anything happen to her. Family members took turns staying with her so that they would always be someone around. The article pointed out that there still was a Mountie security contact, although she had not met with him for five months at that time.

CHAPTER 3: 2000 – ELATION AND HEARTBREAK

A Chance Meeting with Mayor Watson

In early January 2000, I attended a social function and was pleasantly surprised to see Mayor Watson there. I had not heard from him since his email of August 9, 1999, and had no idea how far my proposal had progressed. As soon as he came in and had been greeted by the hosts I approached him, introduced myself and got straight to the point. "How's my Gouzenko plaque project coming along?" I asked. To my satisfaction he remembered it and said it was in his "special projects' file. He was glad to have met me and would pursue the matter.

Subsequently, while trying to keep the poker hot, I sent the Mayor an email on January 9, 2000, saying that it was a pleasure to meet him and that I was happy to hear he remembered my proposal. I further provided some more background about the Gouzenko Affair and quotes from different authorities about its significance. I also addressed the possible plaque location and said that, in my opinion, a plaque should not be erected on the building itself, but in the park directly across the street. As the building was old there was always the possibility that it would eventually be torn down and replaced by something larger and more modern. A plaque on the building itself would be at risk. The posting of any plaques on the building might also attract tourists and disturb the tenants. Instead, I suggested that the plaque should be placed in the park and it would be best if it contained some pictures, including one of the building itself. Thus, if something were to happen to the building, at least the image would survive.

A few days later on January 12, 2000, I received an email from Stuart Lazear, a Senior Heritage Planner at the Department of Urban Planning and Public Works at the City of Ottawa. He addressed me as "Mr. Andrew Kavchek"[sic] and went on to state:

"I have been asked to reply to your earlier enquiry to Mayor Watson and Councillor Arnold regarding the possibility of the City of Ottawa commemorating the events associated with Igor Gouzenko by installing a commemorative plaque at or near 511 Somerset Street West. Mayor Watson, Councillor Arnold and this Department are very supportive of this idea and appreciate your suggesting it. I will now write to the owners of 511 Somerset Street West to solicit their comments and will get back to you once the project comes closer to being realized."

The HSMBC Acknowledges Receipt

Shortly afterwards a letter from Michel Audy, Executive Secretary of the HSMBC, dated January 14, 2000 arrived, stating:

"The Hon. David Kilgour, Member of Parliament for Edmonton Southeast, wrote to the Honourable Sheila Copps on December 29, 1999, regarding your proposal to commemorate the defection of Soviet cipher clerk Igor Gouzenko as an event of national historic significance. Your application, which was included with the Honourable Kilgour's letter, has been forwarded to my office.

I wish to thank you for your time in preparing this submission which is presently under review to ensure that it meets Board criteria for the evaluation of this subject as an event of national historic significance. In the case of a positive outcome of this preliminary review, you will be apprised of when the Board will be able to consider this matter. I will also notify you in the event that your application does not meet criteria."

Although my proposal to Mr. Audy did not generate any response, my approach of getting one Cabinet member to refer the matter to another Cabinet member apparently was working. Some more good news followed, in another letter dated January 25, 2000, from Mr. Audy stating:

"I am writing further to your submission respecting the possible designation of the Gouzenko Affair as an event of national historic significance.

We have complete the review of your application and I am pleased to inform you that your submission will be brought forward for consideration of the Historic Sites and Monuments Board of Canada at its meeting in the Fall of 2000. An historian from the Historical Services Branch, Parks Canada Agency, will be contacting you a few months prior to that meeting to complete your submission."

Finally! Action! At this stage both the City of Ottawa and the federal government were exhibiting positive reactions and moving forward with their internal processes. But why did the HSMBC have to wait until the Fall? I contacted Mr. Audy and was informed that the HSMBC only meets twice a year and it was too late to get this matter on the agenda for the next meeting in June 2000. The meeting in the Fall was either going to be in November or December. In other words, this matter was not going to be brought to a conclusion in 2000. It was becoming evident that this project was going to take a long time.

The City's Attempt to Contact the Building Owners

On March 25, 2000, I emailed Stuart Lazear, asking if the City had any success contacting the building owners. I also inquired about the next steps. A few days later, March 29, 2000, I received the following reply from Mr. Lazear:

"...A letter was sent to the building owners from the Ward Councillor, Elisabeth Arnold. There was no response to that letter and we are currently attempting to contact the owners by phone. Failing this we will proceed with preparing a plaque for installation across the street in the park. The research and design of that plaque would likely be started sometime in the summer depending on other work priorities."

Following-Up with the HSMBC

By May 31, 2000, I had still not heard from the historian at the HSMBC and so I forwarded a letter to Mr. Audy, enclosing a copy of the last chapter from Igor Gouzenko's autobiography titled "Difficult Escape". I requested that the document be forwarded to the historian working on the file, in the hope it would assist them in their research, and generate some activity on a file that I was concerned may have gone dormant.

An Unexpected Lead

On Wednesday, June 28, I came across the Parliamentary Press Gallery website while doing some research on the internet. The website contained a list of journalists and their telephone numbers, including that of John Sawatsky, who had previously written some books about the RCMP Security Service and one about Gouzenko. I called him and asked for his advice. He thought a plaque in the park was a great idea and suggested I get the city newspapers to run a story about how the project was slow grinding because of bureaucratic delays. I was not particularly keen about the notion at that time because I felt that lobbying the media would be just as difficult as lobbying bureaucracies.

Mr. Sawatsky then said something that proved very helpful. He asked "Why don't you ask Svetlana and her family for their support? I'm sure they would give it to you." I thought this was a great idea, but had no idea whether Svetlana Gouzenko was still alive or how to contact the family. Mr. Sawatsky, who had an old phone number from the early 1980s when he was working on his book, gave me the number. I was very grateful. So often I had dreamed of contacting the Gouzenko family, and now I had a lead.

First Contact with the Gouzenko Family

The next day, Thursday, June 29, I dialed the number that Sawatsky had given me. It was long distance to the Toronto area. My heart was pounding as I had no idea what to expect. I planned to ask if I could speak with Svetlana Gouzenko and see what happened. The phone rang several times before a man answered and said "Hello". I asked if I could speak with Svetlana Gouzenko. The person replied "You have the wrong number" and hung up. I was stunned. What could this mean? Did I have the right number, but had not used the right password? Did I make it obvious that I was fishing? Perhaps I reached a number that now belonged to another family and they were sick of hearing the name Gouzenko? I had to find out. So I called the number again, hoping to ask the gentleman whether he had any idea of what had happened to Mrs. Gouzenko. The phone rang and rang, and then an answering machine came on that divulged no information and simply said: "Please leave a message after the beep." I was sufficiently discouraged that I hung up. It was a disappointing failure. Back to square one. I could not figure out how to proceed, apart from calling again later and hoping that someone a little more helpful would answer.

About an hour later, I was sitting at my desk when the phone rang. I picked up the receiver and identified myself. A lady at the other end stated: "You were trying to contact Svetlana Gouzenko", and then asked who was I and what was I calling about. Though puzzled, I immediately began to explain, as quickly as I could, that I wanted Svetlana Gouzenko to know I was pursuing a project to honour her and her late husband. I spoke quickly, as I was scared that if she was a family member she might hang up on me again if I did not get to the point. Fortunately the lady at the other end listened to me and my speed of talking settled down to a normal rate. She heard my explanation and then said "Yes, that is a good idea. We would support that." I asked: "If I may be so bold and inquire, who are you?" She replied: "My name is Evelyn Wilson. I am a daughter of Svetlana Gouzenko".

Bingo! I had made contact with the Gouzenko family. It was a wonderful moment I will never forget. With this success I felt that fate was on my side. Svetlana Gouzenko was indeed still alive and she would now know what I had been trying to do in order to commemorate her and her husband's courage. We exchanged names and phone numbers and I told her that I wished to forward to her my email correspondence. We subsequently discussed a proposal of Ms. Wilson's, namely, whether a letter of support for the project from Svetlana Gouzenko to the municipal and federal authorities would be helpful. I indicated that I thought such letters would help and promised to prepare them.

Shortly after my discussion with Evelyn Wilson (who went by the name Evy) I sent the following email to Mayor Watson:

"This is just a short note to follow-up and inquire with respect to the status of my previous suggestion that the Gouzenko defection at 511 Somerset Street is deserving of a historic plaque... May I ask please how has

the project progressed to date and whether there is anything that I may do to assist in moving it forward?

I managed through some research to communicate today by phone with Igor Gouzenko's daughter with whom Svetlana Gouzenko was pregnant at the time of the defection. She was very happy to hear about this project and sincerely wishes it will come to fruition. It turns out that her mother, Svetlana Gouzenko, is still alive and kicking. Her daughter informed me that she would tell her mother of the project and that she was sure her mother would be very happy to hear about this. Mr. Gouzenko's daughter also asked me how could they assist to complete this project. If there is something we can do please let me know.

I have continued to maintain an interest in this project and hope to see it completed if possible before the end of the year not only to do the right thing but also so that the future transition to another government and structure does not jeopardize this project of such historic value."

The last paragraph was added because the Province of Ontario was forcing the City of Ottawa to amalgamate with the neighbouring cities, to create a new larger City of Ottawa effective January 1, 2001. I knew that such transition inevitably would create some degree of turmoil in the bureaucracy and that the project could be dropped in the event of resource cuts or new priorities.

Following-Up with the HSMBC

On June 30, 2000, I telephoned Mr. Michel Audy to inquire as to the status of the application and his previous statement that a historian would be contacting me to complete the application. He said that the historian would be a lady by the name of Catherine Cournoyer, while her Director was Rick Steward of the Historical Services Branch. Mr. Audy indicated that the next

HSMBC meeting would be in early December and that my application was on the agenda. The deadline for Ms. Cournoyer's report was mid-September, 2000. Eager to learn how her report was coming along, I called and left a message.

Mayor Watson's Message about "Plan B"

On Wednesday, July 5, 2000, Mayor Jim Watson called, while I was out and left a detailed message. He had tried to call the owners of the building at 511 Somerset Street about ten times and failed. There was never any answer and no answering machine. Accordingly, the City would now proceed with "Plan B", namely, putting the plaque in the park.

I wrote to Mayor Watson, that day saying that the "Plan B" option was the best option from my perspective. Furthermore, it made sense, since in his description of the defection, Gouzenko himself stated that there were two RCMP agents on the park bench. I mailed him the letter with two copies of the last chapter from Gouzenko's book, so that he could give it to whoever was working on the city's plaque.

A Visit to Apartment 4

During the evening of July 5, 2000, I returned to the park with my son and strolled in front of 511 Somerset Street. As I waked by, I saw a young man opening the front door. I approached and asked if he could tell me who the building owners were. I explained that I wanted to speak with them, but the front door was always locked, there was no doorbell, nor any sign outside as to who was the superintendent or landlord. He said that the building was owned by two individuals, a brother and sister, and that the brother lived in one of the apartments.

Out of curiosity I asked whether he knew that this was a very historic building and that something had happened here in 1945 which shaped the history of the world. He had heard something about it, that a Russian spy or someone called "Bouzenki" had lived here, but could not find anything about it on the internet. I explained that he may have misspelled Gouzenko's name, which would explain the fruitless search. I related the story and that it all revolved around apartment four. Introducing himself as Ken, he replied that he lived in apartment four and asked if I would be interested in seeing it. He seemed a pleasant fellow, so I accepted his invitation to visit what for me was something of a holy site. I tried not to reveal my excitement.

We went inside and up the stairs to the second floor, where I saw apartments six and four across from each other. I imagined Gouzenko coming home, after being repeatedly rejected, and looking out through the keyhole of the neighbour's apartment as the NKVD broke into his apartment. The door to apartment four had quite a large metal strike plate on the frame of the door where the locks were located. I wondered if those had been installed after the NKVD's visit and survived all these years. Ken unlocked the door to his apartment and I ventured inside. "Wow", I thought to myself. It was an unremarkable apartment in itself, but it will always be one linked to a great event in our history. He provided me with the telephone numbers of both landlords and I thanked him for his kindness and information.

A Conversation with the Landlord

I called both owners that same evening. The first number I called was the brother's. As was the case with the Mayor, there was no response and no answering machine. I called the second number and reached a lady, with whom I had a pleasant chat lasting about half an hour. She informed me that her mother had previously owned the building and when her mother passed away she had inherited it with her brother and her husband.

I discussed the details of the Gouzenko Affair with her and she was aware of the background. I explained that I was pursuing a historic commemorative plaque project and was asking the City of Ottawa and the federal government to erect historic plaques in the park across the street. She indicated that she did not want a plaque on the building for several reasons, including the possibility of tourists disturbing the tenants. However, she had no objecting to putting a plaque in the park. Nonetheless, she would discuss it with her co-owners and looked forward to being consulted by the City.

A Follow-Up Message to the Mayor

The next day I sent an email to Mayor Watson confirming that I had spoken to one of the owners of the building at 511 Somerset Street. I told him that the owner had summarily rejected the City's "Plan A" option of placing a plaque on the building, but did not have a problem with "Plan B". The whole thing made me wonder. In January Stuart Lazear informed me that the City was going to write to the owners. Then in July I learnt that the Mayor has been calling the owners, but without success. How could the City have such difficulty contacting taxpayers? Was my walking by the building that night when Ken was going in a matter of luck or fate?

Mayor Watson Announces his Resignation

On July 6, 2000, Mayor announced he was stepping down as Mayor. The next day, a front page article in the *Ottawa Citizen*, reported he had accepted an offer from the federal Industry Minister to become President and Chief Executive of the Canadian Tourism Commission (CTC). The CTC was established by the federal government, in 1995, to promote tourism in Canada. It had a budget of about $150 million and employed nearly 200 people. By coincidence, the CTC was located in the same downtown Ottawa building where I worked. Even more of a coincidence was that we would be working on the same floor!

With Mayor Watson leaving the scene, I thought it important to ensure that my Councillor be informed of recent developments, as I hoped she would champion the cause at the City to its completion. On July 9, 2000, I sent Councillor Elisabeth Arnold a number of background emails and an update indicating that with the Mayor's imminent resignation, I hoped that I could continue to communicate with her and Mr. Lazear of the Planning Department and provide whatever assistance I could.

On July 10, 2000, Stuart Lazear wrote:

"Thank you for your detective work in tracking down the building owners and determining that they do not want a plaque on their building but would not object to a plaque in Dundonald Park which identified their building. My colleague Sally Coutts will be begin preparing the plaque text later in the summer on her return from holidays."

That same day I replied, thanking him for the feedback and cautioning him that the owners of the building would still like to be consulted in order to avoid any surprises.

A few days later I received an email from Councillor Elisabeth Arnold.

"Dear Mr. Kavchack [sic],

Thank you for the update and your work on this initiative. Mayor Watson indicated to me that he would be following up on the suggestion to install the plaque at Dundonald Park. Should he not be able to complete this project before he leaves office, I will continue to pursue the project with our staff."

Thanking Councillor Arnold for her message, I wrote that the great news made my day. I then forwarded the email to Evy Wilson for her information.

The Gouzenkos Offer their Support

On July 12, 2000, I received an email from Evy Wilson which read:

"We are overwhelmed and thoroughly impressed by your exceptional effort and perseverance in the creation and pursuit of this project. Thank you for sending us your historical e-mail file. It has given us a sense of the scope of the project and the numerous contacts which you have made during the past year. From your well written materials, I have taken the opportunity to prepare a chronology for my mother and to print out and highlight selected correspondence for her to read over. Because she is hard of hearing (a wartime injury), most of our correspondence is on paper. I am working on the proposed letters this evening and intend to mail these tomorrow. If you would like to review the letters prior to sending, please let me know. Your assistance is greatly appreciated in this matter. Indeed it is good news today from Councillor Arnold of Ottawa. We look forward to lending our grateful support to your wonderful initiative."

I responded later that day, stating:

"...I am so very happy that you obtained some satisfaction from knowing that 55 years after the day there are people who wish the memory to survive forever. I appreciate your offer to review the letters, however, I really do not believe that there is such a need unless it is what you would prefer. I would rather not cause any delay and would prefer that you send the letters directly. Would it not be a treat if the plaque was erected on September 5, 2000?

I did not realize your mother had a hearing problem. I was hoping to speak with her someday on the phone. Is that possible? If not, I hope that someday we will meet so that I will have the honour of expressing my admiration for what she did in person.

By the way, today Councillor Arnold misspelled my name as "Kavchack". Similarly, your message misspelled it as "Kravchak". Of course, it is not the first time, and I often wish my last name was an easier Anglo-Saxon name too. I just hope that whoever the artist is that creates the plaque does not misspell your father's name!"

Contacting the Federal Historian

On July 14, 2000, I spoke by phone with Catherine Cournoyer, who would be completing the application to the HSMBC. I had an informative chat with her, then updated Ms. Wilson:

"I just wanted to inform you that I spoke today by phone with Catherine Cournoyer, a historian with Heritage Canada. That was the first time we spoke and discussed the application. She will be working on another project until the week of July 24... Ms. Cournoyer indicated that she will have to write a report for the Board by mid-September. She further stated that the report will have to outline both the good and bad impacts on Canadian history. I asked her what did she mean by "bad impacts". I could see that whatever semblance of McCarthyism that may come about during the late forties and fifties may need to be referred to, however, I am not so sure that such a wide-ranging impact could be said to be attributable solely to the defection of your father. Perhaps Stalin's behaviour in newly occupied lands of Eastern Europe and the rise of Mao, etc....may have had something to do with it. She then referred to some innocent scientists losing their jobs because of poor translations. I am not sure what she is talking about. Nonetheless, her report should be available to us once complete (or at least once considered in December by the Board).

I also asked her how long it would take for the plaque to be set in the park if the Board approves the application in December. She indicated that there is a long backlog and it could take a long time (lack of resources). Thus, I suspect it may take more than a year, perhaps two or maybe more. It seems therefore that we will probably see a plaque raised by the City of Ottawa before Heritage Canada does anything. I did not tell her that I have also pursued this matter with the City because I do not want her to drop the file..."

On July 16, 2000, Evy Wilson replied:

"Thank you for your note describing your contact on Friday with the historian from Heritage Canada. I hope that we have not inadvertently complicated matters... The letters to both Heritage Canada and the City of Ottawa mention "an application to the City of Ottawa...

We too do not want Heritage Canada to drop the file. (Are they not required to approve municipal historical plaques?) The pending report to the Board also raised concerns. The 'cold war' still rages in print. Views of former spies such as Gordon Lunan are freely expressed in recently published books. My father's memoirs, however, remain unpublished. Without the benefit of balance, the public tends to see a very small picture indeed resulting in a bias not based on all the facts. For example, my father was never a spy. Yet in the media and published books, he has been repeatedly referred to as such.

He was in fact a cipher clerk. And, unlike the other members of the embassy, he did not go out within a host country gathering secret data to undermine that country. Under military order and penalty of death, he coded and decoded messages for the Soviet dictatorship engaged in an aggressive clandestine war with Canada and other western countries. The simple goal: to take over. My parents defected months after World War II ended [in

Europe]. Hitler was defeated. Yet the Soviet agents – including Canadian citizens (...among them) – continued to support the Soviet systems. Critical data concerning the withdrawal and redeployment of Canadian troops from Europe were betrayed to Stalin.

We must trust – hope – that Heritage Canada will be both balanced and fair. Above all, they must be accurate. (Could Ms. Cournoyer be referring to recent events in which a scientist released sensitive materials to China? Otherwise, we too do not follow her reference to "innocent scientists losing their jobs because of poor translations". Even those who were convicted following the 1945 espionage exposure and trials later sustained productive careers within the countries which they betrayed. On the other hand, the Soviets imprisoned and often executed people without trial and for the simple 'crime' of being related to someone. Those innocent people lost much more than their jobs).

For decades, the reality of Stalin's terror state was very difficult to communicate to the free world. Now, books about the former Soviet Union some written by earlier spymasters confirm the espionage and the horror which had taken place. Canadians need to know the difference between the perceived "lack of freedoms' in our country today and that which others have endured in Russia and Europe not so long ago.

By the way, there is an insightful documentary which plays from time to time on the Canadian History Channel, entitled 'Man in the Mask'. This film was developed about four years ago and included interviews with a few key people - including my mother - who were first hand witnesses to the historical events of 1945. It may be worthwhile to view. Let me know if you would like to receive a video copy. (I have also painstakingly prepared a transcript of the dialogue for my mother's benefit.)

We wish to have the complete cooperation of Heritage Canada in your wonderful project. In fact, this means as much to us as a commemorative plaque. Their views represent that of our government. All Canadians should be proud of the protective stand which the earlier governments and security agencies had taken during a crucial turning point in our history. Where would we be today if my parents and others had failed?"

I replied to Evy the same day with the following:

"...I understand and agree completely with everything you said. It is such a pleasure to read. I honestly feel of sense of kinship with you and empathize with the difficulty of not having been in a position where you, and others who should know, could respond to distortions of history expressed in public on these cold war issues. I am so glad that we are communicating...

Thank you for sending the letters. I am looking forward to receiving my copies. There may have been some confusion however. I did not mention to Heritage Canada that I was also pursuing a plaque application with the City of Ottawa and vice versa. They do not know about each other's involvement. There are separate applications. If you would be so kind as to provide me with a mailing address (I presume you have a post office box) then I will send you copies of other correspondence I have had with Michel Audy, etc...

In fact, Heritage Canada does not play a role in the plaque installing activities of the City of Ottawa and vice versa. They are separate governments with different mandates and jurisdictions. I pursued an approach last year of applying everywhere in order to maximize the chances of at least one plaque being placed in the park. It is possible that either Heritage Canada may place one or the City, or both (wouldn't that be nice?). If your letter to Heritage Canada mentioned the application to the City of Ottawa, then they may misinterpret it as confusion on your part and think that you are referring to the application to Heritage Canada. If they do subsequently ask me whether there is a separate application to the City then I will tell them the truth of course. Perhaps it would have been best for me to review your letters in advance, but then again, this might all be for the best if Heritage Canada realizes that there is some competition out there and they better hurry up if they want to be first! I only thought that there is a risk that if they believe that the matter has already been officially recognized they may close the file because of a lack of resources. However, that is entirely speculation on my part."

I also told her that I was hoping to meet shortly with the federal historian to discuss the HSMBC application.

On July 19, 2000, she sent the following email:

"...I shall go ahead immediately. The letters are now drafted and will be presented to my mother early this afternoon. If all goes well, the correspondence will be in the mail today or Friday at the latest. Copies will be sent to you by regular mail. As well, and with your agreement, I would like to forward copies of your key correspondence to those individuals who have been supportive in the past. They may be helpful in this project.

It would be truly exciting to have the memorial plaque in place on September 5th. For over fifty years, we have met wonderful people who understand and acknowledge the true issues associated with the defection. Sadly, there are those who do not share that understanding. I cannot easily comprehend their motivation. We live in and enjoy a country with freedoms which mankind has seldom enjoyed throughout its long history. These freedoms are worth protecting. Every Canadian should know it.

My apology for the misspelling of your name. Actually, it was a typo error was missed on re-read. My fingers tend to append an "r" before an "a". Over the years, my father's name has been misspelled repeatedly, for example, 'Guzenko'. Thus, when I scan the indices while researching materials, I check in several places. I've retained my married name Wilson throughout my adult life, making things just a little bit simpler.

While my mother has difficulty hearing, she nevertheless enjoys conversations when others speak loudly – although not by phone. We hope to have the pleasure to meet you one day soon."

Shortly afterwards I received in the mail copies of two letters of support to Michael Audy and to Mayor Watson, each signed by Svetlana Gouzenko. In both letters she stressed that she and her family were pleased to learn recently of my applications for a plaque to commemorate the Gouzenko defection of 1945. The letter further stated that she and her family were most grateful and willing to provide any required assistance.

Mayor Watson's Commitment

The Mayor of Ottawa replied to Svetlana Gouzenko in a letter dated July 20, 2000, with a copy to me.

"Dear Mrs. Gouzenko,

Thanks very much for your kind note. I am pleased that you approve of our plan to commemorate the "Gouzenko Defection" of 1945.

Ms. Sally Coutts of our Heritage Branch has been assigned to the task of producing the plaque and supervising the unveiling, which will take place later in the Fall.

As my term as Mayor ends on August 14, Councilor Elizabeth Arnold, who represents Somerset Ward will help to carry through with this very worthy project.

I thank you for your letter and I am most appreciate of Andrew Kavchak for his assistance with this very historic and exciting project.

Sincerely, Jim Watson Mayor of Ottawa"

I almost hit the ceiling when I read that letter. A commitment from the Mayor to unveil the plaque in the Fall of 2000 (just a few months away!). This was a major milestone. If everything went according to plan I would hopefully be able to meet Svetlana Gouzenko at the unveiling ceremony. If had now been one year since I started pursuing this project. This letter marked a point of no return. If I could convince the Mayor of Ottawa to share in the vision, then I realized that this project had a chance. From this day forward I would do whatever I could to make it a reality.

Evy Wilson Receives HSMBC Feedback

On July 26, 2000, the following email arrived from Evy Wilson. She had received my package with copies of relevant documents, as well as a reply from the HSMBC to her letter of support.

"At last we have received the parcel. As I write, my mother is reading through the correspondence. Thank you so very much for your tireless effort. She is thrilled. The letter from the Historic Sites and Monuments Board of Canada is very promising. Because I do not have a scanner, I shall paraphrase the essence of the text from Michel Audy:

'I am writing at this time to thank you for your letter of July 11, 2000, in which you kindly support Mr. Andrew Kavchak's nomination of the Gouzenko defection of 1945 as an event of national historic significance.

A copy of your letter has been provided to Ms. Catherine Cournoyer of Parks Canada's Historical Services Branch, who has been assigned the responsibility of preparing the historical research paper on this subject for the consideration of the Historic Sites and Monuments Board of Canada (HSMBC). As requested, you will be kept apprised through Mr. Kavchak of the outcome of the HSMBC's deliberations once the Minister of Canadian Heritage has had an opportunity to review the Board's recommendations on this matter...'

Andrew, we thank you for making this possible. I hope one day that your efforts will be rewarded..."

I replied to Evy Wilson the same day with an email in which I stated that it gave me a lot of satisfaction to know that they were now able to enjoy these events as they unfolded.

Meeting the Federal Historian

On July 28, 2000, I met Catherine Cournoyer at a coffee shop at the corner of Bank and Somerset, just a few blocks away from Dundonald Park. I brought with me several books relating to Gouzenko to show to her. She gave me a binder with standard forms and explanatory notes for the Submission Report for an Event to the HSMBC. Ms. Cournoyer and I then walked down Somerset Street to Dundonald Park. Across from 511 Somerset Street we stood and discussed the events which had transpired there in 1945. She took some photographs of the building, but ran out of film and said she would have to return.

Ms. Cournoyer was a recent history graduate from a Francophone university in Quebec. From my discussion with her I got the impression that her knowledge of Gouzenko was lately acquired. One aspect of our conversation, which I found disappointing, was her insistence on addressing the negative aspects of the affair. In my opinion, the fact that individuals were supplying classified information to the Soviet Union, at a time when it was led by one of the most cruel and murderous dictators in history, was the negative aspect. Gouzenko's revelations and the government's awakening from its chronic somnambulism were the positive aspects. I was hesitant about what kind of a report she was going to write and wondered whether it would make any difference if a more senior historian had been assigned to the file. I hoped that if her report was dismissive the Board members would be sufficiently knowledgeable to compensate for any shortcomings.

Exchanges with Evy Wilson

In an email on August 1, 2000, Evy Wilson informed me that she had received the Mayor's letter and that it was very encouraging. She then added:

"...when should Heritage Canada be advised of the decision by the City of Ottawa? We are looking forward to the federal government report – although it may take them months to produce. Would they consider a coordinated effort with the City? Please let us know your thoughts."

I responded to her later that day:

"... It sounds like great news from the City – there does not seem to be any test to pass now – it seems to have been assigned to someone and should take place in the Fall. This is fantastic news!

Concerning telling Heritage Canada, I would rather hold off for now. I am not sure that they need to know at this time, or any. The fear I have is that they find out that the City is putting up a plaque they may reconsider and drop the project on the basis that the event has already been commemorated. They may not, but the thing is that they keep repeating that they have little resources, and accordingly they may use that as a reason to drop the file. I am only speculating, but I would prefer to wait until after the City has already put up a plaque. Heritage Canada will likely contact the City anyway to obtain permission to put the plaque in the park. At that time they will find out (if they have not already learned by then). Let's keep our fingers crossed and hopefully the City will put a plaque in Fall (before it gets too cold) and then maybe next year Heritage Canada will put up an even bigger one. I doubt they would consider a coordinated effort because each has a separate mandate and such coordination would unnecessarily delay things. Please remember that the City and the Region of Ottawa-Carleton will be reorganizing on January 1. I hope that the plaque will be installed before then because there will be a loss of municipal jobs and this project may risk falling between the cracks if it is not completed by then. Those are just my thoughts though, who knows how these bureaucracies will evolve?..."

Following-Up with the City

On August 2, 2000, Tara Peel, an assistant in Councillor Arnold's office, sent an email to Sally Coutts, the person to whom Mayor Watson stated that that the file had been assigned, which read, in part:

"I am writing to follow-up on Mayor Watson's July 20th letter to Svetlana Gouzenko on which both you and Councillor Arnold were copied. In his letter, Mayor Watson indicates that you will be producing the heritage plaque and supervising the unveiling for 511 Somerset Street West. Please keep Councillor Arnold informed of the progress on this, and let me know if there is anything that this office can do to facilitate the completion of this project."

Thanking Councillor Arnold and Sally Coutts, the same day, for their messages, I informed them that Mrs. Gouzenko was thrilled by Mayor Watson's letter. I asked that they consult with her on the plaque wording once a text was drafted. The email generated an "Out of Office AutoReply" to the effect that Sally Coutts would be absent until August 14. I forwarded my original email and the "autoreply" to Evy Wilson, so that she would know where matters stood. For the time being, they stood nowhere. The next day Evy Wilson replied, stating that she appreciated the correspondence. I had no idea at that time just how many more emails this project would generate.

Initial Contact with Ms. Coutts

On September 1, 2000, I called and spoke with Ms. Coutts and got an overall picture of where things stood now that she was back at work. The City, apparently, received two to three proposals a year to erect a plaque to commemorate the defection of Igor Gouzenko. These suggestions were usually made by university students, but never resulted in anything. In this case, however, it was being done because the former Mayor wanted it done. Thus, I was glad that I had forwarded my application to him. Even though the letter from the Mayor had indicated that it was to be done in the Fall, it was her intention to have it done by December 31, 2000 (i.e. possibly in early Winter). The plaque would be an interpretative panel similar to the one recently unveiled at the Millennium Fountain in the market area, which contained an explanatory text, as well as a series of old pictures of the area. The Gouzenko plaque would have a bilingual text of approximately 1,000 words, as well as photographs. Ms. Coutts was going to do the research for the plaque text herself, and was going to visit the National Archives and obtain some photographs to insert in the panel. The text was to be geared towards the average person and point out that Igor Gouzenko was a key figure. However, it would not be too politically detailed and focus instead on his heroic act. It would be simple and a salute to him. Since Ms. Coutts was only starting her research, I told her that I had an annotated bibliography with relevant excerpts received from the Gouzenko family which I proposed to send to her.

When I asked about the design of the plaque, she said that the work would be done "in house". Thus there was no need to go through a tender process to have it made by an outside company. She further indicated that manufacturing of the plaque would take a few weeks and that the base of the plaque pedestal would be installed in the ground during the Fall before the frost set in. She also planned to work with the landscape architects.

When I queried about the procedures and approvals and whether anything else was required or had to be done she indicated that nothing else was necessary. While other matters needed City Council's approval, this one did not (there was a push to get other matters before Council prior to the elections in November). As the first email from the Mayor in 1999 indicated that he was going to discuss it with City staff, I presumed that a full year later the process and requirements had been discussed and were being complied with.

Drafting the Plaque Text

A few weeks later I suggested to Evy Wilson that, since Ms. Coutts was only beginning her research and it was already Fall, perhaps it would be helpful if we were to submit a proposed first draft of a text for the plaque. After all, no one knew the Gouzenko story better than the Gouzenko family. If they were to supply a first draft, then clearly it would save some time. My experience has been that a first draft of any text is often the hardest to write and so I believed that we would be doing Ms. Coutts a favour and helping to move things along to meet the deadline. I drafted a proposed text and forwarded it on September 14, to Evy Wilson, with the hope that she and her mother would make whatever changes they felt were necessary and then send it to Ms. Coutts.

"... What follows is a text that I would very much appreciate if you could look over it and make any changes you wish. As you will note, there are a

few specific spots where I put some question marks because I hope that you can fill in the blanks... I hope you like the text. Please remember that Sally Coutts did not want it to be too political, but instead to focus on the courageousness of your father. Also, it should stick to the facts and be written as a story for the public... It is supposed to be about 1,000 words. I did not count, but if we offer a little more, she will be able to edit.

Please forward your amended version to me and I will forward to Sally Coutts. Alternatively, of course, you may forward it directly to Sally Coutts yourself. To be honest, I would actually prefer that. I think it would give some extra credibility to the text which I cannot provide. Let's face it, you and your mother know what you are talking about.

With respect to your email to me, I can confirm that neither Ms. Coutts, nor Ms. Cournoyer at Heritage Canada, have either thanked me for forwarding the bibliography or even acknowledged receipt. I find that truly disappointing, however, they both told me in previous discussions that they were very busy. I would suggest that you send the text, after you have amended it to your satisfaction, to Sally Coutts. (Please copy me on the message). I will then call her a week or so later to follow-up and see how things are coming along. Please do not send it to Heritage Canada yet as it would be too premature given that they will only have their board meeting in December (They are slower than molasses!).

I also met this week with Jim Watson, the former mayor and now Director of the Canadian Tourism Commission... I asked to meet with him so that I could express my gratitude and tell him how happy you were about the possibility of the panel being erected (since Ms. Coutts told me that the project is only being pursued because he wanted it). He told me that he was very pleased but regretted that it has been taking so long! He hoped it would have been completed before he resigned last month."

Evy Wilson was receptive to my idea and spent the weekend with her mother working on the text. On Monday, September 18, she forwarded the draft text to Ms. Coutts.

"We have been in touch with you through your e-mail address by Mr. Andrew Kavchak of Ottawa who has spear-headed this wonderful project. My mother, our family and I are deeply honoured by this gesture of the City of Ottawa. We are hopeful that Canadians will gain a better understanding of the events which shaped our country during the past century and helped to maintain our democratic way of life. Many individual sacrifices were made in that quest.

I firmly believe that the security of our country cannot be a partisan issue. We must work together to ensure that the truth and vigilance prevail in matters of maintaining and improving our basic human rights and freedoms worldwide. Unfortunately, all tyrants are man-made.

Enclosed, please find our draft text proposed for the historic plaque. Andrew had kindly prepared and sent us a first draft last Thursday from which we carefully revised sections during the weekend. The result is a text of slightly over 1000 words which accurately reflects the facts and the impressions of someone who has lived through these events. While I understand the wish for the text not to be too political, my mother has some difficulty with this concept. The events were/are political in nature and aftershocks are still felt today. My mother cannot easily dismiss Stalin's tyranny and the terror she has experienced in her lifetime. We hope that you will like her draft text and find that you are able to draw a final text from it.

We have also appended a number of quotations which may be of value, in particular, that taken from the Royal Commission Report of 1946. As well, we had prepared and forwarded to you through Andrew an annotated bibliography of selected references on the topic. We have other materials which we would like to forward to you by mail in the near future.

In the meantime, we look forward to hearing back from you via this internet address. I am Svetlana's eldest daughter (born at Camp X) and am in direct contact with her."

Shortly afterwards, Ms. Coutts replied with an email, the tone suggesting that she did not appreciate our unsolicited attempt to assist. I had the impression that we had inadvertently offended her and was fearful that our attempt to be helpful and save time had backfired. I then communicated with her and tried to explain that it was only meant to be helpful. Fortunately, this unanticipated hurdle was overcome and Ms. Coutts proceeded to work with and edit the submitted draft text.

Following-Up with HSMBC

On September 29, I called Catherine Cournoyer and left a message asking how the project was coming along, whether she finished her report, etc. I was hoping to see a copy of her background report to the HSMBC, which was supposed to supplement my application and make it complete. Unfortunately, I was not given a draft of the report to comment upon, nor did I see the report before it was considered by the HSMBC.

The City Edits the Proposed Plaque Text

On October 16, 2000, Sally Coutts sent Evy Wilson an email with an attachment containing the second draft of the proposed plaque text. The email stated: *"As you can see, I simplified and shortened the very informative text that you sent me in late September. Work is progressing on the panel and I have arranged to have its base installed in the ground before the deep frost."* She further indicated that she had ordered several photographs for the plaque. She added that she assumed Ms. Wilson was Gouzenko's daughter and asked her for comments on the latest draft of the text. She concluded by saying *"I look forward to hearing from you as quickly as possible so I can initiate the design process."*

Two days later Evy Wilson sent a reply to Sally Coutts which read, in part:

My Mother and I would like to thank you for your very kind letter of Monday, October 16th and the attached copy of the proposed text for the panel. She has read over the draft and is very pleased with its overall accuracy and the sense of the event. A few minor adjustments are suggested below with further edit down the length of the text. She fees that the 'banner' (ref. Statement from the Royal Commission Report of 1946) is best suited at the end of the panel highlighted and separated from the main text. We do have pictures – photos and original art work – which you may find of value for the panel. These will be forwarded to you by the end of the week for your consideration.

I am Igor and Svetlana's eldest daughter born at Camp X – and on paper carry the name Gouzenko in which we were awarded our Canadian citizenship. My older brother, Andrei Gouzenko, was born in Ottawa while our parents were part of the Soviet embassy staff. The rest of my brothers and sisters (there are many) were born under the assumed name given by the R.C.M.P. Our father, however, never received identification in his assumed name and our mother only after our father's death in 1982.

Sally, thank you for this opportunity to take any active part in the development of the honorary panel..."

The rest of the email contained a few suggested modifications to the text. Evy Wilson forwarded the package of emails and attachments to me on the same day with the following note:

"Ms. Sally Coutts, City of Ottawa sent us an e-mail on Monday evening. With it, she had forwarded a draft text of the panel for our review. I am enclosing our reply and a copy of her original e-mail. Once again, thank you for your tremendous initiative and for the very first draft of what now will appear (hopefully) as the final text for the panel. As a family, we are extremely proud of this honour and have much for which to thank you."

My response to Evy Wilson the next day contained the following:

"... when I spoke to Ms. Coutts about 5 weeks ago she indicated that she would provide us with a copy for comments, and I was clearly under the impression that it included both you and me. However, she has not communicated with me at this point. Of course, if you are satisfied with the proposed text then I really doubt that I would have any concerns...

Thanks again for your receptivity and support of this project. Imagine how sad I would be if you were against it!"

Sally Coutts subsequently made some more editorial changes and forwarded the third draft of the plaque text to Evy Wilson. The latter responded to Sally Coutts on October 26:

"It's beautiful, concise, factual, readable, and politically correct, the final text nicely conveys the theme which you have intended. We (our family) are truly grateful for this positive recognition and honour...

Please bear with my mother's "use of Cold War rhetoric". She is correct in her experience to acknowledge what was taking place in Canada at that time. It was far more sinister than the simple act of spying or 'an exchange of information' as many pundits have implied. It was high treason against Canada, the U.S. and Great Britain. The unbridled purpose was the secret infiltration and overthrow of democratic countries by the Soviet dictatorship. One country after another was being consumed by an underground army of revolutionaries who maintained direct allegiances to the Soviets. These issues, however, are addressed by my mother and father in their respective memoirs which we hope one day will see the light of print. Correctly, such harsh realities do not belong on the panel..."

When Evy Wilson forwarded this third draft to me, we hoped it would be the final one.

City Bureaucrats Delay Project

During my frequent walks past Dundonald Park I could see no evidence of a plaque foundation being installed. I waited for news and finally on November 20, 2000, called Ms. Coutts and asked her whether a date had been set for the unveiling ceremony. To my dismay she informed me that there were be no plaque unveiling that year, but that it had been decided to postpone it to the Spring of 2001. Not only were things very busy at City Hall with the pending amalgamation, but a Spring unveiling would have the advantage of a better photo ops, since it was getting increasingly colder. According to her, it would be no problem to erect the plaque in April. The previously agreed to text was being translated and she had ordered some pictures, including one picture of Igor Gouzenko with his trademark hood, from the National Archives. Ms. Coutts further indicated that she had informed Councillor Arnold and the Gouzenko family and they had respectively agreed to the delay.

I was terribly disappointed with this news. Svetlana Gouzenko was an elderly lady and her presence at the ceremony would have been a photo op beyond description, even if held on a cold day. Although she could have attended a ceremony in the Fall of 2000, to delay it would be taking obvious risks. Who knew how her health would hold out? I expressed great disappointment at this turn of events and at not being informed or consulted. Had I been asked I would have opposed any delay. She dismissed my concerns by saying that she thought the Gouzenko family would have told me. I suspected this bad news was a harbinger of worse things to come. Once a delay is introduced, bureaucrats can always find reasons to extend it.

I had my own concerns about how the decision was likely presented to the Gouzenko family. I subsequently asked Evy Wilson about what she was told. She confirmed that they consented to the delay and believed that I had known about the City's decision. She was surprised when I made reference to the new unveiling target of April, 2001, as she did not recall a month being mentioned. I suggested that the delay was very bad news and requested that if such developments occurred again, to categorically oppose them.

On December 17, I emailed Councillor Arnold to comment on the progress (or lack thereof) to date and made a plea concerning future consultation.

"... While I realize that there is much work involved in such a project (which is why I tried to help by writing a text and also supplying a bibliography) I would like to say that I am very saddened and disappointed by the delay. I am also extremely saddened that when the delay was raised and discussed that I was not informed and consulted. I also regret your approval of the delay.

I would like to ask that you please consider doing the following:

Please monitor this file to ensure that the historic plaque is installed in April and no later. Ms. Gouzenko is an old lady now and may not live to see the day.

Please also inform me of any significant events on the file when they occur. Although I would also like to be consulted and asked for my opinion, at least being informed would be sufficient. I am just an individual citizen who made the suggestion. I have no personal interest in the project apart from a love of history and a feeling that this recognition of a significant event in Canadian history is long overdue.

For your information, in the Fall one evening I noticed a large CBC movie truck filming the location of 511 Somerset Street. They parked several vintage cars in front of the building to add authenticity to the defection. Apparently they were filming to be part of the history series that should air next Fall. Even the CBC recognizes the significance of the place and the event..."

A Horrible Year-End: the HSMBC Postpones its Review

At this point in time I figured that at least there would be some progress on the federal side. The HSMBC was scheduled to meet in early December of 2000 and my application was on the agenda. Unfortunately, a letter from Mr. Audy, dated December 28, 2000, shattered this hope.

"... The HSMBC was not in a position to evaluate this submission at its December 2000 meeting as it had a number of other pressing items to review in a limited amount of time. As a result, the Gouzenko Affair has been brought forward to the Spring 2001 meeting of the HSMBC.

I hope that this change in scheduling has not inconvenienced you in any way, and thank you in advance for your patience in this matter..."

70

What a disappointment! First the City said they would put it up in the autumn, then delayed it to the following Spring. Now the HSMBC had my application for over a year and would not even be considering it until their next meeting in June 2001. Although I had reason to be optimistic earlier in the year, the situation now seemed bleak.

The letter from Mr. Audy was also a good specimen of bureaucratic communications practices. Only civil servants can refer to a delay as "bringing forward". While I appreciated being thanked in advance for my patience, I only wish someone would have honestly told me how much was going to be necessary. I also wondered what were the "pressing items" to which his letter referred. Perhaps the letter was a sign that I should press a little more myself.

CHAPTER 4: 2001 – RED TAPE AND THE PASSING OF AN ICON

Following Up with the HSMBC

After receiving Mr. Audy's letter, I called his office to find out more about future timing, but he was away, so I left a message. I forwarded a copy of his letter to Evy Wilson. On January 17, 2001, Mr. Audy called and indicated that my application would not get bumped from the agenda of the next HSMBC meeting in June. The HSMBC would then forward a recommendation to the Minister, who should decide approximately three months afterwards. Thus, it was possible that the Minister could make an official historic designation before the end of the year. The process afterwards involved negotiating with the City for space in the park, but if the City did not agree the HSBMC would consider alternative sites. He added that the wording of the plaque should reflect the reason it was of national importance and the Gouzenkos and I would be consulted on the wording.

Picking Up Where the City Left Off

On January 1, 2001, the City of Ottawa amalgamated with neighbouring municipalities in the former Regional Municipality of Ottawa-Carleton to create the new City of Ottawa. Bob Chiarelli was elected Major and Councillor Elisabeth Arnold was re-elected.

On March 12, I received a call from Evy Wilson. She had moved six weeks earlier and had not reconnected her computer. I gave her an update, which was short, since nothing had happened recently. I asked if she was going to come to the unveiling ceremony, and she indicated that she and her mother were interested - but would decide later.

On March 27, I sent an email to Councillor Arnold and Sally Coutts. My family had changed internet services providers, so I wanted to inform the City of our new internet email address, and I added:

"Also, for your information, in the past several months there have been a number of articles in the media about the apparent defection of a Russian diplomat in December and the subsequent exposing of a long-time FBI agent in Washington, etc... It is interesting to note that while many of the articles suggest that this is the first major defection in Ottawa since Gouzenko, they also say that Gouzenko's impact was more significant."

Several days later on March 30, Sally Coutts replied:

"A date has not yet been set for the panel unveiling but it will be late April or early May. The details of the unveiling are not being arranged out of this office. Please contact Councillor Arnold's office for that information."

Councillor Arnold Submits a Request

The day before, March 29, Councillor Arnold sent an internal City written memo to Lesley Donnelly, Corporate Communications. I received a copy in the mail a few days later. The memo's subject line was "Plaque Installation at 511 Somerset St. W." It read as follows:

"Over the years, my office has received a number of requests for the City to recognize 511 Somerset St. W., the home of Mr. Igor Gouzenko, a cold war defector in 1945. Mr. Gouzenko in his position as a Clerk for the Soviet government learned of Soviet intelligence operating several spy networks in Canada. Mr. Gouzenko defected with his family, bringing with him documentation outlining the extent of Soviet espionage in Canada.

Sally Coutts has been arranging production of a heritage plaque to be installed at this address with the assistance and approval of Mr. Gouzenko's family and other community members who have been working diligently towards this event. Ms. Coutts is prepared for the plaque to be installed this spring in late April or early May.

I request that Corporate Communications coordinate this plaque unveiling with the assistance of Ms. Coutts, and invite Mayor Chiarelli to this event."

I was thrilled that she had taken this initiative. At this stage I still hoped that the plaque might actually unveiled in April or May 2001.

On April 8, I emailed Leslie Donnelly at the City of Ottawa, suggesting the name of one federal government official who I believed should be formally invited to the plaque unveiling ceremony. I thanked him for his work on the project and asked that he not hesitate to contact me if he had any questions or information about the unveiling. A reply arrived the following day:

"... While your thanks are very much appreciated, they should actually be directed to Brigitte Mineault. Brigitte is co-ordinating this project for Communications and Marketing and, as you have noted, is doing an excellent job. I work directly with the Councillors and Brigitte works on

projects such as yours. She will be in touch with you soon to work out the next set of details."

The fact that someone actually had a full-time job at the City working on projects such as mine was good news as it meant that the City had some experience and familiarity with the issues and process. Later that day I emailed Brigitte Mineault the following:

"... I would like to thank you for your work on this project. Please let me know the date and time of the planned unveiling when you have them. If you would like to discuss any details with me, please feel free to call me at my office... Alternatively you may contact me by this email address to my home.

One thing I would like to stress however, is that while I did make a plaque proposal two years ago, it is my understanding that over the years many people have done so. I do not have any particular interest in this project apart from a love of history and a belief that it is long overdue. Accordingly, I do not want to have my name mentioned or recorded anywhere with respect to this project and wish to remain entirely anonymous. If any speeches are to be made I hope they will not make any reference to me. This is about Gouzenko's courage, and what he and his wife did for the Western world which I, and many others, admire. As I suggested in several emails, it seems to me that the heads of the RCMP, CSIS and the Ottawa City Police should be invited to the unveiling, as their organizations were involved and owe a great deal to Gouzenko..."

Concern Over the Nature of the Ceremony

In the weeks that followed I had several telephone conversations with Ms. Mineault in which the primary issue addressed was the nature of the ceremony. In keeping with the Gouzenko family's historic and ongoing security precautions, Ms. Mineault had offered to organize a private plaque unveiling ceremony, where only members of the family and selected guests would be invited. The media would only be informed about it afterwards.

To me this whole ceremony issue was an unnecessary complication. When the City made reference to an unveiling ceremony for the "photo op", I mistakenly assumed there was no choice, even though the risk was that the Gouzenko family would not attend. If they did attend, they were not likely to identify themselves and deliver any speeches. However, Ms. Mineault's proposed option of a private ceremony may have been the perfect compromise.

Unfortunately, the City did not propose a date for the ceremony to the Gouzenko family and ask them which of the two options they preferred (public or private) along with a deadline to reply. Instead, I continued to liaise with Evy Wilson by telephone and email and asked her which option they preferred and if she could reply to the City. Unfortunately, her family was going through a particularly busy period and it took her approximately two weeks to contact the City. I was not particularly surprised that it took two weeks to indicate the family's preferred option. After fifty-six years of hiding and staying out of the public eye one could expect that the consideration of options for the participation in a public commemorative ceremony of this nature would justify some reflection. Nonetheless, Evy Wilson communicated by phone with Brigitte Mineault and confirmed that the family agreed to the plaque unveiling ceremony being a public ceremony in which the family members who attended would remain anonymous individuals in the crowd.

I waited for the news, as to the timing of the ceremony, but heard nothing. Messages left for Ms. Mineault were not returned. Finally, on June 26, I called Brigitte Mineault for an update, only to be informed that she would be away until July 3. Even though I left another message, it was not returned.

I subsequently called Mayor Bob Chiarelli's office and left a message with his scheduling assistant. I indicated that I had been told that a date for the ceremony would be set once the Mayor's attendance could be confirmed. I stated that the contract person I had been dealing with had not been returning my calls and now appeared to be on vacation. Accordingly, I asked if she could tell me whether the Mayor had received a request to attend the ceremony and whether he had confirmed his participation on any particular date.

An ensuing call from an extremely irate woman who gave me quite a brush-off and told me that I had no business calling the Mayor's office, stunned me. This project was getting weirder by the minute and I was starting to think that City Hall was a truly dysfunctional organization. Nothing seemed to be real over there. Letters and memos from our elected representatives were consistently ignored, phone messages were not returned, all worked stopped as civil servants went on vacation. Now I was told that I had no business calling to inquire about what was going on.

On June 29, I sent the following update to Evy Wilson:

"I thought you might like an update on the situation with the City's unveiling of the plaque. I would also like to make a request of you to contact them again.

About three weeks ago I sent an email to Brigitte Mineault at the City and then to my Councillor Elisabeth Arnold to ask for a status report. They did not reply.

So a few days ago I called and left a message for Brigitte Mineault. Her voice message said she was away until July 3. So I called her colleague in her absence and he knew nothing. He said he would tell her that I called. I also called my Councillor's office and they did not know what was going on and said they would call me later. They did not.

I also called and left a message for the Mayor's office asking the scheduling assistant whether the Mayor has indicated a date yet. Would you believe that I just received a very nasty call from the Mayor's office saying I should be dealing with Tara in Councillor Arnold's office… The person from the Mayor's office said she spoke with Tara who indicates that "there is some sort of problem with the family". So I called Tara and left her a message, but they were gone for the weekend.

The bottom line is this: every time the City has options (e.g., timing of the unveiling, or nature of the ceremony) it is a grand source of confusion and excuse for delay. If they provide you with any future choices please make the simplest one right away and do not give them an excuse to postpone. Although you provided them with your response on the ceremony issue (i.e., that it could be public) a month ago, it appears that the only person who knows that is Brigitte Mineault. She did not tell Councillor Arnold's office and it appears that the Mayor's office has not been asked to attend the ceremony and provide a date for availability. In fact, they are under the impression that there is a "family problem". Do we not have enough problems with the City's bureaucracy without giving them any further reasons for delays? This is really turning into a disappointment. Nonetheless, we have come too far to give up now…

May I kindly ask that you please contact Brigitte Mineault as soon as possible and reconfirm that your family wishes to have the plaque put up as soon as possible and that a public ceremony is OK. Similarly, could you also please contact Tara in Councillor Elisabeth Arnold's office… and tell them that you already informed the City that your family is OK with the idea of a public ceremony and that you would like to know when it will happen.

If I do not get any satisfactory answers within the next week or two then I may send the Mayor a copy of Mayor Watson's letter of last year indicating that it would be done by the end of 2000 and then the letter from Arnold asking that the event be organized now, and I may ask him to more the project forward. I can't believe that this has been ongoing since August of 1999..."

Several days later Evy Wilson responded with an email, saying that she was just as surprised as I that the City made a reference to a "family problem". She promised to contact Brigitte Mineault and thanked me for my efforts.

Following-Up with the HSMBC

In early July, I called Mr. Audy to find out where things stood with the HSMBC, then sent the following email on July 4, to Evy Wilson:

"Guess what? I called Michel Audy at Heritage Canada... and I got the update at the end. Fortunately, it is good.

It appears that the last meeting of the Commission took place June 14-16 in Charlottetown. Apparently, they considered my application to have your father's flight to freedom declared an event of historic significance. They made a recommendation to the Minister. Mr. Audy could not tell me what the recommendation was, but I would be surprised if it was negative. Mr. Audy says it will take around 4 months for the Minister to receive the recommendation and make a decision. I will receive a letter informing me of the Minister's decision afterwards. Maybe in November/December. Hopefully the recommendation and the decision will be positive. If that will be the case, then it will take another two years to set up the plaque, but at least we know it will be done.

The bottom line: A major and significant hurdle has been overcome. This is progress."

Back at the City

On July 17, I called Brigitte Mineault again and found out that this time she was on holidays, as were several of my other contacts. Of those who were in the office, none knew anything about the file status. However, one of Mineault's co-workers, Mike Brule, told me that he would try to check the file and get back to me. He returned my call on July 20, and told me that the plaque was done, though there appeared to be some outstanding legal issues regarding the unveiling ceremony. He speculated that the City might opt for a private ceremony rather than a public one. I said that that was fine with me, but that I would like to see this ceremony occur sooner rather than later. I could not believe that we were getting held up over the form of a ceremony. All I had proposed was a plaque. When I asked who was Brigitte Mineault's boss he referred me to Andrea McCormick, Manager, Development Services. The messages I left for Brigitte Mineault were not returned.

Thereafter, I called Ms. McCormick and eventually had a discussion with her on August 7, which was pleasant and businesslike. She said she had just received the file and seemed to think an unveiling ceremony was unnecessary. While the City gave an undertaking to erect the plaque, it might dispense with the ceremony because of the privacy concerns for the family. She asked me for Evy Wilson's phone number so that she could speak with the Gouzenko family, even though the file should have already had that information. After talking to Evy Wilson she would update me with regard to the unveiling plans.

A Bureaucrat Vetoes the Mayor

When after two weeks I had not heard from Ms. McCormick, I called and left a message. After playing telephone tag, we finally connected on August 20. What she told me was a complete reversal from our previous conversation. She stated that she had researched the matter and could not figure out why the City had planned to unveil a plaque. She had spoken with several other persons at the City who told her not to do it and she was not going to proceed with the planning and unveiling of the Gouzenko plaque primarily for procedural reasons. Ms. McCormick did not tell me who she had talked to or what positions they held. She went on to say that the newly amalgamated City was developing a new commemoration policy, but until it was finalized and formally adopted, the policy of the old City of Ottawa was applicable. She claimed it had not been followed. Because of the international dimension of the Gouzenko Affair, the Department of Foreign Affairs and International Trade (DFAIT) would have to be consulted. In addition, the plaque proposal required City Council's approval. Since the Gouzenko plaque application had not gone through this process, she claimed the former Mayor did not have the authority to issue a commitment for the City to erect a plaque.

Again, as when I spoke with Sally Coutts the previous November, I became numb with shock. The City had this file for two years and it was increasingly clear that nobody there knew what they were doing. I informed Ms. McCormick that I had previously discussed the City policy with the Mayor and Sally Coutts and it did not correspond to what she was describing. She was adamant and would not budge, simply dismissing the matter and bringing the conversation to an end by saying she was sorry that it had come to this. Before the conversation ended I asked her to put her decision and reasons in writing and send me information on how I should proceed with my application in accordance with these newly-discovered procedural rules. Ms.

McCormick agreed to do so. I also asked her if she had called the Gouzenko family, as she previously had indicated she would. She had not.

After hanging up the phone I reflected on this news with disbelief, and regretted how much time had been wasted. After two years, the file had the misfortune of landing in the hands of someone who resorted to procedural arguments to block the project and made the absurd suggestion that employees of the old City had improperly ignored their own procedures. The City of Ottawa now looked inept. Considering that Ottawa is the nation's capital I found the situation embarrassing.

While waiting for Ms. McCormick's letter I reflected on my options. I was already drafting new letters in my mind and thinking of contacting the media to see if they would be interested in another case of bureaucratic bungling. It raised the question of who was in charge at City Hall. It appeared that bureaucrats were vetoing decisions of elected officials with impunity. What did this say about democracy in Ottawa? Things, I thought, could not get much worse.

Following my conversation with Andrew McCormick, I wrote to Evy Wilson:

"I have some bad news. I received a call today from Andrea McCormick at the City who informed me that the plaque project will not go ahead. Apparently, although she told me two weeks ago that she would call you, instead it appears that she decided to consult with a lot of other bureaucrats who told her that there is a policy that for such a plaque project with an international dimension they need to get instructions from all of City Council and to consult with External Affairs. I told her that we have a letter from both the Mayor and the Councillor. If there is a policy that all of Council needs to approve it and that External Affairs needs to be consulted, then why did the Mayor send the letter? Why was the policy kept a secret from him and

from my Councillor? We had a discussion in which I expressed profound disappointment and indicated that the way the City dealt with this was very unprofessional. She agreed and regretted the events. I asked her to send me all this information in a letter. I want to have a record of it... Apparently, what would now be required, is for an application to be made to the City Council, with more documentation. I told her that this should have been explained two years ago, not now. She informed my councilor last week, but I have not heard anything from her... Well, we still have a chance with Heritage Minister Sheila Copps. Hopefully, the recommendation from her Historic Board will be positive and so will be her decision. I should receive a letter from her in October or November. If it is positive, I will be relieved. If it is negative, I will be very sad, for it will prove that 10 years after the end of the USSR, Canadian politicians are still scared of the Russian communists."

The Receipt of More Sad News

Two days later I received a disturbing email from Evy Wilson.

"We have sad news too. Our dear mother is very ill. The news you send at this time is very sad indeed. Thank you for your valiant efforts. These matters are much bigger than us. I shall be in touch with you as soon as there is an opportunity. Please keep this news confidential..."

The situation was looking bleak. The City had blocked the plaque project and now that Svetlana Gouzenko was very ill, it was unlikely she would ever see it. On top of it all, the Federal government bureaucracy was so slow that it would almost be a miracle if a federal plaque was unveiled any time soon. However, even if it was unveiled the next day, it appeared unlikely that Mrs. Gouzenko would have been in good enough health to make the trip to see it. I was further saddened by the fact that I would now be unlikely to meet my hero in person.

Death of an Icon

By September 7, I had still not received Ms. McCormick's letter, so I called and left a message. No response. On September 10, I contacted former Mayor Jim Watson at his CTC offices and gave him an update on the project. I informed him about Ms. McCormick's claim that he had not followed old City policy. He responded that he had the authority to make the decision he made and that it sounded to him like policy was being developed "on the fly". He promised to check the status of the file with Councillor Arnold and see whether it could be resuscitated. He regretted he had not "fast tracked" this project as he brought to my attention the newspaper articles that day. Svetlana Gouzenko had died!

I was stunned when I heard the news, and immediately obtained newspapers to confirm. My worst nightmare scenario had become reality. It happened on September 4, 2001, just one day before the anniversary of their defection. She was 77.

I had dreamed of meeting this courageous lady and witnessing her presence beside the commemorative plaque, but two years lead time was not enough to get it done. I wished I had known earlier of Mrs. Gouzenko's passing, because I would have been able to deliver a timely letter of sympathy. However, the family was obviously busy and I was not in the inner circle. Indeed, although I had many conversations with Evy Wilson and regularly exchanged emails, we had never met. Upon reading the newspaper articles confirming Svetlana Gouzenko's death I sent Evy Wilson an email expressing my deepest regrets.

I also called Mr. Audy that day and left a message pointing out that Svetlana Gouzenko had passed away on September 4, 2001, and suggested that this information be added to the HSMBC file. Later that day he called and confirmed that it would be a footnote in the memo to the Minister. He reported that the matter was going through the necessary internal procedural hoops and that the critical stages had apparently been completed.

The next day, on September 11, 2001, approximately one hour before the twin towers of the World Trade Centre in New York City were struck by terrorists, Evy Wilson sent the following email:

"Thank you for your kind note. The funeral was held in Mississauga yesterday in our mother's 'protected' name which is carried by many of my brothers and sisters and their children. We are planning to have a memorial service for both my mother and my father in their real name in the near future (2-3 months). At that time, a headstone will be placed at last at the gravesite retaining the true name "Gouzenko" and an appropriate epitaph. For almost twenty years now, our father has had an unmarked grave. Andrew, we would be honoured if you and your family would be able to attend this ceremony. More information will be forthcoming in about a month."

I was very touched by this email. As the location of burial site was a closely guarded secret, I felt it would be a privilege to attend such a ceremony in the company of the Gouzenko family and to see the location where my heroes were resting. I thanked Evy for the message and replied that I would be honoured to attend.

One More Time... Can I Get That in Writing Please?

By September 12, Ms. McCormick's letter had still not arrived, nor had she returned my phone call of the previous week. Accordingly, I called again and left a message asking when I could expect to receive her letter. I also mentioned that Svetlana Gouzenko had just died and that there were articles about it in the papers. I added that I would appreciate a reply and that previous messages had gone unanswered, which I considered "unprofessional".

The next day Ms. McCormick called to say a letter would be in the mail to me that day. It arrived September 18.

"Further to my conversation with you, I am writing to let you know the actions I have taken re: the request for a commemorative to honour Mr. Gouzenko. I do apologize for the delay that has occurred in communicating these actions to you by telephone on August 20 and the follow-up letter.

Prior to our conversation in August, I discussed the status of the City of Ottawa's recognition policy with the Innovation & Development Branch of our People Services Department.

This Branch plans to recommend a new policy to Council in 2002. In the absence f the new policy, the former City of Ottawa's policy is being used to assess requests. Basically, the nominee's contribution is reviewed with a view to determining the extent of his/her municipal contribution, followed by a report and resolution to Council, if appropriate.

Given that Mr. Gouzenko's contribution is international in nature, you may wish to pursue this request with Foreign Affairs or the Historic Sites and Monuments Board of Canada or you may wish to provide your comments on the scope of the new City of Ottawa policy to Josée Helie, Manager of Policy and Planning for the Innovation and Development Branch of the People Services Department.

Councillor Elisabeth Arnold has been advised of the status of your request. Should she wish to pursue this further with Council, we await that advice..."

The letter was copied to Councillor Elisabeth Arnold, Josée Helie, and Sally Coutts. I was disappointed with the letter's lack of detail and the extent of omission of what she had told me back on August 20, namely, that the previous Mayor had no authority to make the commitment to unveil a plaque without consulting with DFAIT and getting Council's approval. Also, the letter contained some new information about the review of "municipal contribution". This was the first I heard of this criteria. The first significant international incident of the Cold War happened in Canada's capital city and I could now see the City using the lack of a "municipal contribution" as an excuse for permanently shelving the plaque project. On top of it all, it provided no indication as to whether there was anything I could do to get things going at the City. Instead, the only possibility of the file being resuscitated depended on whether Councillor Arnold would take the initiative. That same day I delivered a copy of the letter to former Mayor Watson with a note stating:

"...please find enclosed a copy of a letter from a city bureaucrat who effectively vetoed your decision of last year regarding the Gouzenko plaque on the basis of some procedural policy. Do you have any advice on how I should proceed, or is it a hopeless case...?"

Shortly after, I received a phone call from Mr. Watson saying that he had called Councillor Arnold's office and spoke with her assistant, Tara Peel. The process, outlined in Ms. McCormick's letter, did not reflect the policy as his bureaucrats explained it to him, when he was Mayor. He added that, given this obstacle, maybe the Federal route was not the way to go. I informed him that I had been pursuing the federal route through the HSMBC, since the beginning, but that they were just as slow, if not slower, than the City. However, Mr. Watson hoped that the red tape at the City could be cut and this matter straightened out. He was optimistic and hopeful.

That same day I called and left a message for Councillor Arnold, asking her to return my call. This would be the third time in the past month and a half that I left a message hoping that someone would call. That afternoon Tara Peel returned my call. She had no idea that there was a problem, nor had she received a copy of Ms. McCormick's letter. Ms. Peel said that they would look into it and get back to me that week.

I was so annoyed about the situation that I called Sally Coutts. I wanted to gauge her reaction to the letter of Ms. McCormick which she was copied on. As she was not in, I left a detailed message saying that Ms. McCormick's letter contradicted what she had told me the previous year. I asked if she could explain the contradiction on procedural policy. I also informed her that Svetlana Gouzenko had passed away and would be unable to participate in any "photo op".

Several hours later Ms. Coutts called back and left a voice message saying that she had not received Ms. McCormick's letter. She was under the impression the previous Mayor did not need to get the Council's approval. The only way to explain the situation was that the present Mayor had a new policy (even though McCormick's letter stated that there was no new policy and that the old one had to be followed). Ms. Coutts then assigned blame for the delay in the plaque unveiling ceremony on the Gouzenko family, for not knowing what kind of ceremony they wanted. The plaque was ready and could be installed any time. Finally, she made it clear that she did not have anything to do with the file and stated that I should deal with Ms. McCormick from then on. Assigning the blame for the delays on the Gouzenko family struck me as unworthy. The indecision of the Gouzenko family regarding their preferred ceremony option caused, at most, a two week delay. Given that the City had the file for two years it was an exaggerated claim, to say the least.

After hearing Ms. Coutts message I immediately called Ms. McCormick to inform her that her letter of the previous week did not appear to have been received by the people it was copied to, who worked in the same building. She indicated they were being distributed internally that afternoon. I explained that I wanted to move forward with this file pursuant to her newly discovered policy and do whatever was necessary to get the plaque erected. The person who could walk me through the procedural policy would contact me that afternoon, or at least I would be contacted and told who it was. The lack of professionalism at City Hall continued that afternoon. Contrary to what she told me to expect, no one called.

I sent Evy Wilson an email updating her on the latest developments in this fiasco. I suggested that since the City of Ottawa was being so difficult perhaps a more appropriate place for the federal plaque would be her parents' gravesite. By the way the City of Ottawa was dealing with this matter I was starting to think that Dundonald Park was not a fit and deserving location for such an important symbolic item.

Councillor Arnold Picks up the Ball

On September 21, I called Tara Peel in Councillor Arnold's office and she confirmed that their office had finally received Ms. McCormick's letter. She informed me that Councillor Arnold had asked for a meeting with Ms. McCormick and wanted to proceed with the erection of the plaque. If there were some procedural hoops that had to be overcome, Councillor Arnold wanted them clarified and to proceed. Ms. Peel also said that instead of commemorating the person, the initiative consisted of commemorating the heritage aspect of the building. This would give a greater legitimacy to the municipal claim of commemoration, rather than risk failure on the basis that it was not municipal enough in nature. However, if a motion before Council was necessary, Councillor Arnold was prepared to support it. Ms. Peel confirmed that she would keep me informed with updates. This was good news to me. Although it had taken more than two years, and the ball had been fumbled many times, it was still in play. The action might be in reverse, but I was still hopeful that we could score a touchdown before my son graduated from high school.

By October 4, I had not yet heard from Ms. Peel, so I called for an update. Councillor Arnold had had a meeting with City staff who were not willing to move on the file. Consequently, she was seeking further meetings with other bureaucrats to find a process. Councillor Arnold was prepared to submit the plaque project to Council for approval, but wanted to ensure it would not be defeated by paving the way in advance (e.g., if consultation with the Federal government was necessary, then that would have to be done first).

In late August, after the negative verbal news from Ms. McCormick, I had drafted a very critical letter about how the City had completely botched this file. However, as Councillor Arnold appeared to be pursuing the project as best she could, and given the opposition this project was encountering, I decided to hold off with the letter for the time being.

Following-Up with the HSMBC

On November 9, 2001, I called Mr. Audy and left a message asking for an update. His answering machine indicated that he was away that week. On Thursday, November 22, I called him again and left another message. I finally received a voice message from Mr. Audy indicating that on Tuesday, November 20, 2001, the HSMBC conducted a final review of the submission, which would now proceed to the Minister for her consideration. He could not tell me what the HSMBC's recommendation was, nor could he say when the Minister would make a decision. I was thoroughly perplexed by this message. On July 4 and September 10, I was told that the Board had dealt with my application at its June meeting and that it was proceeding to the Minister. Now I was told that the Board had just completed a final review and the file would only now proceed to the Minister. I did not follow up to clarify this inconsistency, as making contact was not easy. I often felt that the less I knew, the better I slept at night.

The City Consults with DFAIT

On November 22, I received a voice message from Jim Watson saying that he had bumped into Sally Coutts who reported that Councillor Arnold was intent on pursuing the plaque project. Mr. Watson suggested I call Councillor Arnold and ask her office to pursue it and call him back in two weeks if nothing happened, as he might have some other ideas. So I phone Ms. Peel in Councillor Arnold's office and left a message asking her to call me back. I subsequently called and left another message on November 26, but my calls were not returned.

Two weeks later, on December 10 I had a telephone conversation with Ms. Peel, in which she informed me that Josée Helie, Manager of Policy and Planning, was working with the Office of Protocol to liaise with DFAIT. Apparently a consultation letter was going out to DFAIT, if it had not gone out already. Since the City was now consulting with DFAIT, I informed Ms. Peel of my application to the HSMBC. I told her that when I received word about Minister Copps' decision, I would let the City know as soon as possible.

With regard to consultation with the federal government, I could not figure out why the City of Ottawa chose to only consult with DFAIT. It seemed to be a setup for disaster. DFAIT's position at best would be neutral. I could not see them being enthusiastic about a plaque to honour a Soviet defector, and I could easily imagine them opposing it in order to avoid the risk of receiving a complaint from the Russian Embassy. DFAIT could use the excuse of not wanting to offend the current Russian government. On top of it all, Gouzenko exposed a spy at External Affairs, so this chapter in the

Department's history was not its finest hour. There were other federal Departments with whom the City could have also consulted. Besides the obvious one of Heritage Canada, there were the Departments of Justice, Solicitor General, National Defence, or a central agency such as the Privy Council Office. However, even though the City was not going to consult with any other Department, by informing Ms. Peel that the Heritage Minister was going to make a decision regarding a historic designation, I had effectively put the City on notice that another federal Cabinet Minister was going to be making a decision on this very issue. Unfortunately, it did not appear to matter.

CHAPTER 5: 2002 – A DEATH BLOW AND SAVING GRACE

Following-Up with the HSMBC and the City

On January 25, 2002, I called Michel Audy hoping for an update but his voice message said he was out of the office. So I called another person in his office by the name of Mario Savard. I filled him in on Mr. Audy's voice message of November 22, 2001, and explained that I was confused as to the status of the file. Was final approval given by the Board in June or in November? Was the Board's recommendation with the Minister? I hoped Mr. Savard would be familiar with the details or at least offer to check, but instead he suggested I wait for Mr. Audy's return.

On February 18, I called Ms. Peel for an update and she said that DFAIT was still reviewing the matter. She indicated that there were now a number of commemorative options on the table, unveiling of a plaque being just one of them. Apparently the Office of Protocol and Manager Josée Helie were continuing to work on the matter.

On March 5, I called and left a message for Mr. Audy, who was away that day. On March 22, I left another message, asking him to call me with information on the file status. That afternoon he called, only to say that the

Gouzenko recommendations had not gone to the Minister yet. Hopefully they would by June. Apparently the HSMBC had not made a recommendation to the Minister at their meeting in June, 2001. The Board members determined that they needed further clarification as to the reasons for the national historic significance of the event and the wording of the reasons and sent it back to the Board's Secretariat. To say I was disappointed was an understatement. Though the HSMBC first received my proposal in November, 1999, it now appeared that the background paper prepared for the Board was inadequate to assist it in making a decision. I believed that the Gouzenko Affair was not only well known, but of such obvious importance, that I was stunned that so much time was required to deal with it. Concerning the future, Mr. Audy informed me that the Record of Minutes of the meetings are usually about 70 pages long and those from the last meeting of November 2001 were being finalized and expected to be forwarded to the Minister the following week.

National Archives and the Sharing of Information

I called Evy Wilson with an update, while she shared with me some interesting new developments. After her mother's death, she was contacted by the National Archives interested in acquiring her parents' documents. She expressed some concerns and referred to the way my applications had been poorly treated by the bureaucracy. National Archives then contacted Heritage Canada to find out what was happening with my application. Heritage Canada responded by sending National Archives an email confirming the positive recommendation of the HSMBC at its latest meeting, as well as a copy of the research paper their historian had prepared. The National Archives then sent a copy of this email and the paper to Evy Wilson. Even though I was the person who submitted the application, I was told that I could not be informed of the recommendation of the HSMBC until after the Minister had made a decision, and I was not offered a copy of the historian's research paper. Ms. Wilson promised she would send the texts to me which I received on April 10, 2002.

The HSMBC Background Report

The Background Report on the Gouzenko Affair prepared for the HSMBC's consideration was a 21-page document in French and had my name on the front page as the person making the proposal. The report gave an overview of the event and an assessment. It concluded that the event constituted the introduction of the Cold War to Canada, since it raised the awareness of Canadians to the real nature of relations with the Soviet Union. The document ended with a discussion of possible locations for the plaque and suggested Dundonald Park. While the report attempted to present an accurate reflection of the historical record, I was not entirely satisfied with it. I felt it was bland and certain details, such as the context, were missing or not sufficiently elaborated on. In my opinion, the text neither recognized the Gouzenkos as the courageous heroes they were, nor adequately reflected the significance of the events and consequences. I was also concerned about some of the report's secondary sources, which struck me as having a bias. I did not bother to critique the document or forward any commentary to the HSMBC, as they had made a positive recommendation for the historic designation of the Gouzenko Affair. The file was now on its way to Heritage Minister Sheila Copps and I would have to wait until she announced her decision on whether or not to accept the HSMBC's recommendations.

DFAIT Asks the City for Details

On April 18, I called Ms. Peel for an update. She had nothing to say, except that she would follow-up and send me an email. By April 23, I had received no communication so I sent a lengthy email to Councillor Arnold. I pointed out that, although I was very happy that she pursued the project after Ms. McCormick effectively vetoed the Mayor, it had now been seven months since she wrote her letter. I had not received a single letter or email from her offices confirming the process being pursued or the corresponding timetable to bring the project to completion. I requested that she do what she could to ensure that the plaque be erected without any further unnecessary delay.

The following day I was copied on an email from Tara Peel of Councillor Arnold's office to Josée Helie.

"I am writing to see whether there is an update on the status of this issue. Councillor Arnold was recently contacted by a resident who is keenly interested in having this move forward, as it Councillor Arnold and I indicated that I would follow-up to see where things stood. Any update you can provide would be appreciated. Thank you."

The email had a trail of three short emails below it. The first was dated January 11, 2002 from Bernadine Clifford, Acting Protocol Officer of the City of Ottawa, to Elisabeth Arnold stating:

"This is to advise that staff at the Department of Foreign Affairs and International Trade (DFAIT) are reviewing background information on the request to commemorate the defection of the Gouzenkos in 1945. They will advise us of any reason(s) why the City should not proceed with plans to commemorate. I will keep you apprised of the situation."

The second email, dated February 1, was also from Bernadine Clifford to Councillor Arnold and read as follows:

"I just wanted to provide you with an update on the status of the request to commemorate Mr. Igor Gouzenko. As you know, background information was sent to the Department of Foreign Affairs and International Trade (DFAIT) earlier this month. Staff at DFAIT have advised they are busy with preparations for Team Canada to visit Russia in February. As such, they have asked that this request be postponed until March, after Team Canada returns to Canada.

Staff have indicated they would like more time to consult with their specialists in Russia. They have also asked for more details about the event, including the type of commemoration, date, time and location, etc. Please let me know if a draft proposal for the commemoration has been prepared."

The third email was form Ms. Peel of Councillor Arnold's office to Bernadine Clifford dated February 7. It read:

"... Thank you for the update on where the consultation with DFAIT stands. In terms of the details around the commemoration, those are currently undetermined. In terms of the actual commemoration, we had decided to have a plaque installed in Dundonald Park across the street from the property at 511 Somerset Street West. There have been a number of different proposals for how to proceed with this ranging from a press conference to a quiet installation of the plaque in Dundonald Park. Plans for the commemoration have been suspended for now, because the City's Communication and Marketing Branch indicated that the consultation with DFAIT was required before we could proceed. If you have any proposals for the commemoration, Councillor Arnold would welcome the opportunity to review them."

After receiving the above message I felt compelled to write to Councillor Arnold on April 24:

"Thank you for forwarding these emails to me. I appreciate the background information. Any further future update would be appreciated.

However, I would like to point out something. There are several ways to look at what may be commemorated, it could be the person, the event, or the place. In fact, what is unique to the City is that a dramatic and very significant event at the start of the cold war took place in downtown Ottawa at 511 Somerset Street West. Why on earth DFAIT would have to consult with "specialists" in Russia is beyond me. What are they going to do in Moscow that they cannot do here?

The emails… do not seem to have a clear and consistent message about what is being considered for commemoration. In one email it is the "defection of the Gouzenkos" while in another it is simply to commemorate "Mr. Gouzenko". What about the historic event at a historic location in Ottawa?

In addition, I am surprised that the DFAIT staff asked for more information about the time, date, location and type of commemoration. When I made my initial proposal to the City I never suggested that there should be a ceremony or big public event. When Ms. McCormick asked me last year why is a public unveiling and media event being planned I replied that it was the City's idea and not mine and that I would prefer that there not be one. If DFAIT is concerned that a public event to attract attention may be excessive then I agree. Please tell them that the erection of a three foot high plaque does not have to be a media event."

Meanwhile, Over at Heritage Canada

On May 23, I contacted the HSMBC again for an update. I ended up speaking with Michelle Pilon, an Information Officer. She informed me that we could expect an announcement regarding the Minister's decision on the recommendations of the HSMBC "within a month".

The City Clerk Delivers a Death Blow

The month of May passed without event and then a bombshell fell in my mailbox on June 17, 2002. It was an envelope from the City of Ottawa. It looked very formal, and since I had not received anything like this in a long time, I sat down as I opened the envelope. It was a good thing I was sitting when I read the letter. Inside was a two-page letter from the City Clerk dated June 6, 2002 (it took 11 days to get to me even though I lived only eight blocks from City Hall).

"This is to inform you about the City of Ottawa's decision with respect to the request to commemorate Mr. Igor Gouzenko and his wife Svetlana for their efforts during the Cold War. I apologize for the time it has taken to resolve this issue, and would like to provide you with a summary of the process that was followed.

In a letter dated 12 September 2001, Ms. McCormick, Manager of Marketing and Communications at the City of Ottawa, advised that the former City of Ottawa's policy would be used to assess your request. This would involve reviewing the nominee's contribution to determine the extent of his/her municipal contribution. If deemed appropriate, the result of this process would be outlined in a report to Committee and Council.

Given that Mr. Gouzenko's contribution was of an international nature, Ms. McCormick recommended that you might wish to pursue this request with the Department of Foreign Affairs and International Trade (DFAIT) or the Historic Sites and Monuments Board of Canada.

On 17 October 2001, your request was forwarded to the city of Ottawa's Office of Protocol for direction. The Office of Protocol contacted the Deputy Chief of Protocol and Director of the Diplomatic Corps at DFAIT with a request to advise us on this matter.

After consultation with their specialists in Russia, staff at DFAIT advised that from the point of view of international relations, the Department did not find it appropriate to commemorate this episode of the Cold War. While they acknowledge that the City of Ottawa is solely responsible for deciding on the recognition of an individual's contribution to the City of Ottawa or to municipal history, they hoped that the City would consider their concern regarding this issue.

After careful consideration, staff at the City of Ottawa recommended that we not proceed with plans to commemorate Mr. Igor Gouzenko.

Sincerely,

Pierre Pagé
City Clerk / Director Secretariat Services"

The letter was copied to Mayor Chiarelli, Councillor Arnold, Cathy Bowles, Chief of Protocol, and Jim Watson.

Given the length of time the process was taking I had prepared myself for a possible negative outcome. Nonetheless, I was profoundly shocked and disappointed upon reading the letter. Nearly three full years of lobbying had come to nothing. The bureaucrats had managed to defeat a former Mayor's commitment. In the three years that I had lobbied the City, I had never been invited to attend a meeting to discuss the file and had never met any of the bureaucrats.

I was still waiting for a decision from the Minister of Canadian Heritage. There was still hope that the federal government would come through if the Minister of Heritage was concerned about our heritage. I was exhausted and chose to wait with my response to the City until I heard from Sheila Copps. If she agreed, there would be at least one plaque, on behalf of the whole country. Depending on her decision, I would either throw in the towel, or have the last laugh.

I then called Evy Wilson and gave her the bad news. She asked to see the wording, so I typed the letter into an email and sent it to her. I concluded my email with the following paragraph:

"... While we are fighting a war against terrorism we refuse to acknowledge and thank those who risked their lives to save our freedom 57 years ago. Of course, I do not suspect that the Russians toned down their funeral celebrations for Kim Philby for fear of harming relations with the West, but that evidently does not matter. Our only hope left is with Sheila Copps. I was told that a decision could be made as early as this month. Well, it is already the 17th and I am still waiting."

Evy Wilson responded the next morning.

"... We too are very disappointed by the decision of the City of Ottawa to discontinue the historical plaque project. The 'Soviets' still wield considerable power in Canada. Please do not consider your magnanimous efforts a loss. In fact, you have single-handedly brought to light a crucial weakness in our political mindset. The former 'Soviets' still have the ability to influence decisions even at the municipal level. Misinformation abounds..."

Heritage Minister Sheila Copps to the Rescue!

On Monday, July 15, 2002, I tried to call Mr. Audy. However, he was on holidays until August 8, so I left message for his co-workers. A little later that day I spoke with Michelle Pilon. She took my address and said that the Minister's office had indicated that the Minister could make a decision and sign off on the recommendation of the HSMBC "this week".

On the morning of Friday, July 19, Ms. Pilon called to confirm my fax number and to say that something could happen soon, possibly that day or on

Monday. Then at 12:04 p.m. I received a fax. The cover page said that "Attachments will follow by mail." The one page faxed letter was on the Minister's official letterhead and dated July 19, 2002. It read:

"I am pleased to advise you that I have recently designated The Gouzenko Affair (1945-1946) an event of national historic significance.

When it met in November 2001, the Historic Sites and Monuments Board of Canada considered the national significance of the Gouzenko Affair and recommended its designation. An excerpt from the minutes of that meeting is enclosed for reference. Should you want a copy of the research paper prepared for the Board's consideration on this matter, you can contact M. Michel Audy, Executive Secretary of the Board, by telephone.

Preparations for a plaque unveiling ceremony entail consultation with you and other interested parties regarding the plaque text and other logistical matters. This process usually takes at least 18 months. Mr. Doug Stewart, Field Unit Superintendent, Eastern Ontario, or his representative, will advise you as plans for the event are developed. For further details, you are invited to contact Mr. Stewart by telephone.

In view of their interest in this matter, I have forwarded a copy of this letter to the Solicitor General of Canada, the Minister of Foreign Affairs, the Member of Parliament for Ottawa Centre and the Ontario Minister of Culture...

Yours sincerely,
Sheila Copps"

Ms. Copps had no idea how happy she had made me. I immediately called Evy Wilson with the news. I only wished we were in the same room because I would have like to give her a congratulatory hug as if our team had just won the Stanley Cup, the World Cup of soccer and an Olympic gold medal all in one shot! This was a moment of great satisfaction, relief and excitement for both of us. Suddenly, I felt that all the effort had been worthwhile. I was also amused that copies of the letter were sent to the Minister of Foreign Affairs, Bill Graham, and the M.P. for Ottawa Centre, Mac Harb. The Minister may not have known of the previous recommendation of his staff, but at least he would know of his fellow Cabinet Minister's decision and that it was a *fait accompli*. Similarly, I wondered whether Mac Harb continued to believe that I should still be dealing with the City and that my proposal had nothing to do with the federal government.

I called Ms. Pilon to thank her and let the staff there known just how much I appreciated this. She indicated that she could forward me a copy of the research paper that was prepared for the HSMBC. The Heritage Canada News Release was posted on the Heritage Canada website about an hour later. I appreciated their courtesy of informing me first.

The Heritage Canada press release of June 19, 2002, was titled "Minister Copps announces Historic designations in Canada". Nine new designations of national historic significance were announced. Five were persons, four were places and the one event was the Gouzenko Affair. However, for each of the nine designations there was a separate "Backgrounder" document. The "Backgrounder" for the Gouzenko Affair read as follows:

"The Gouzenko Affair (Ottawa, 1945-1946)

The Gouzenko Affair, which revealed the existence of a Soviet spy ring in Canada, is an event of national historic importance. For Canadians, it marked the beginning of the Cold War and an awakening of anti-Communist sentiment. Indeed, it made Canada, as well as other nations, recognize the changing relationship with the USSR and the chilling of the world's political climate. The Gouzenko Affair sparked legal proceedings and a Royal Commission in Canada, becoming a milestone in the debate on State security and civil liberties; in the long term, it resulted in the restructuring of the national security system.

The Affair began in September 1945, shortly after the signing of the peace treaty with Japan. Igor Gouzenko, a young officer posted to the Embassy of the USSR in Ottawa, defected on September 5, carrying with him 109 secret documents revealing the existence of a Soviet spy ring in Canada, particularly within the federal public service, and reporting that results of atomic bomb research might have been leaked to the Kremlin. The Government of Canada immediately place Gouzenko and his family under protection and Mackenzie King apprised his British and American counterparts of the situation. The three heads of state (King, Attlee and Truman) decided to keep the affair secret until conclusive evidence could be collected.

However, in February 1946, the Gouzenko Affair burst into the open, perhaps through a leak from the American government. The news quickly made world headlines and King hastily set up a Royal Commission. For one week, the Commission pored over the documents handed over by Gouzenko and, on February 14, it recommended the arrest of some of the individuals mentioned in the documents. The following day, thirteen suspects were arrested and the government announced this fact. The Commission then began a more in-depth inquiry; it was given sweeping powers to detain suspects and strip them of their rights. The Commission's report was made public on July 15, 1946. It reported that a Soviet spy ring had been operating since 1924, drawing the link between Soviet espionage activities and the global Communist movement, and found nine other Canadians guilty of espionage. The Commission's report recommended that the government tighten its security measures and more closely control access to positions of trust within the public service.

For a long period of time, the Gouzenko Affair remained vivid in the collective imagination of Canadians, even more so since Gouzenko himself was always seen as a mystery. For the rest of his life, he maintained this mystery by covering his face during public appearances."

I got home that afternoon and to find a large envelope had been delivered by courier. It consisted of the letter signed by Sheila Copps, which I had received by fax at the office. It also included a one-page excerpt of the minutes from the November 2001 meeting of the HSMBC, which was not part of the fax received at the office earlier that day.

"Supplementary Report: The Gouzenko Affair, Ottawa 1945-1946

Background

The Board considered the Gouzenko Affair at its June 2001 meeting and was prepared to recommend this subject for designation as an event of national historic importance. Before forwarding its recommendation to the Minister of Canadian Heritage however, the Board asked that Parks Canada provide further information about an appropriate location for the commemorative plaque and clarify questions related to national historic significance.

Recommendations

Designation: The Board recommended the Gouzenko Affair for designation as a National Historic Event to be marked by a standard commemorative plaque at Dundonald Park in Ottawa.

Statement of Significance: The Board recommended the Gouzenko Affair for designation because

The discovery of a Soviet spy network in Canada was a defining moment in Canadian history marking Canada's entry into the Cold War and generating anti-Communist sentiment among Canadians;

it exposed Canadians and citizens of other countries in the Free World to the changing nature of relations with the USSR and marked the cooling of the world political climate;

the judiciary procedures and the Royal Commission that resulted from this affair represent benchmarks in the debate on Canadian civil liberties and state security; and

it resulted in the long-term development of a formal state security system in Canada."

I was somewhat puzzled by the four reasons given as the statement of significance that justified the historic designation. There was no mention of the drama of the defection or Igor Gouzenko's courage. There was no mention of the defection and its aftermath constituting one of the first significant international incidents of the Cold War. The primary issue was the exposure of the government's vulnerability and the extent to which it was penetrated by Stalin's agents. Thus, it seemed to me that the reference to state security should have come first. I thought that the matter of the changing relations with the USSR was a poor choice of words because, even though the Soviets had on occasion switched tactics (e.g., joining Hitler to start WWII), their objectives from the time of the Russian revolution remained the same, i.e., to supplant all political systems, including liberal democracy, with communism. Thus, to suggest that there was a time of warm relations with Stalin struck me as somewhat naïve.

Similarly, with respect to representing benchmarks in the debate on civil liberties and state security, it seemed to me that the primary revelation of the affair was the vulnerability of the state, the Soviet penetration of it, and the corresponding need to strengthen the state's security. The debate and concern over the treatment of the suspects after the defection, and the legal rights that they were afforded, was certainly important, but in the context of the overall affair, was it more significant and deserving to be mentioned ahead of state security? It is interesting to note that while critics have suggested the spy trials were "show trials", only half of the suspects were convicted (unlike the "show trials" in the Soviet Union where the evidence was fabricated and the outcome predetermined). Nonetheless, I felt that the outcome was what counted. I was so relieved that the Minister had made the historic designation that I was not about to quibble over the HSMBC's wording.

The following Monday July 22, 2002, an envelope from Ms. Pilon arrived containing the research paper prepared for the Board. Although I already had received this from Ms. Wilson, the package from Ms. Pilon contained a supplementary six page report in French, with an elaboration of possible locations to place the historic plaque. Six locations were identified, including Dundonald Park, the Justice Department building, an RCMP building, the East Block of Parliament Hill, the location of the former Soviet Embassy, and Camp X. I found it ironic that DFAIT and the City of Ottawa had rejected the idea of erecting a commemorative plaque to honour Gouzenko, on the basis that it could offend the Russians, yet the HSMBC report considered placing such a plaque right in front of the Russian Embassy![17]

---

[17] The former Soviet Embassy was destroyed in a fire in 1956 and replaced with a new building. After the collapse of the Soviet empire the building continued as the location of the Russian Embassy.

Let the Media Coverage Begin!

There was nothing in the press over the weekend, but on July 22, the media started producing a series of daily articles in newspapers across the country, which lasted several weeks. Over the weekend Evy Wilson had been in contact with Ann Marie Owens, a *National Post* reporter, who sought the reaction of the Gouzenko family to the news. She mentioned that an individual in Ottawa had spearheaded this project. Ms. Owens had wanted to contact me, but I had previously asked Ms. Wilson not to reveal my name for the time being and she respected that. She had sent me an email on Sunday, July 21, about her discussion with Ms. Owens and concluded by saying *"Once again, my family and I congratulate you on your profound success. We are very pleased that this journey has brought us to a worthwhile destination."* And the journey was not yet over!

The article in the *National Post* on Monday, July 22, 2002, was titled "Clerk who revealed spy ring wins historic designation" and contained two photographs of Igor Gouzenko, one hooded while being interviewed by a journalist and one without the hood when he was a young man. The article began with the factual statement about the Minister's historic designation and then it went on to state:

"The Gouzenko Affair, as it is known in the official designation and in newspaper reports of the time, helped shape the psyche of the generation of Canadians who lived through the Cold War, but also resulted in the longer-term reshaping of the national security system... Ms. Wilson said her father and mother believed strongly they had a duty to warn the West about the dangers of Russian espionage... Although the government's official designation has an important symbolism for the Gouzenko family, Ms. Wilson says "the ultimate relief" will come when she can make contact with relatives in Russia, who were exiled in punishment..."

On July 22, Mr. Michel Audy sent Evy Wilson a letter, informing her of the Minister's decision, which also contained the Supplementary Report.

A Swipe at the City

All day long on July 22, I took great satisfaction in reflecting on the *National Post* article and the long journey to this point and the road ahead. I wondered whether I should bring this to the attention of the bureaucrats at the City of Ottawa, who had just last month rejected my application after three long, turbulent years. However, at the time, I felt so discouraged by the City's decision that I merely wanted them to be aware of the fact that the Federal government might wish to put up a plaque on City property. I had not conceived of asking it to reconsider. I was so exhausted by the shenanigans at the City that I did not want to go through that kind of ordeal again. Finally, at the end of the day, at 4:48 p.m., I sent an email to Councillor Arnold, Mayor Bob Chiarelli, Pierre Pagé. Benadine Clifford, Andrea McCormick and Jim Watson. The email read as follows:

"Further to my proposal to the City of Ottawa in 1999 about the possibility of the City's commemoration of the significant events that took place in 1945 at 511 Somerset Street and the former Mayor's, Mr. Jim Watson, letter to me of 2000 indicating that the City would unveil a plaque in Dundonald Park before the end of the year (and also further to Andrea McCormick's letter of September 12, 2001 and Pierre Pagé's letter of June 6, 2002 contradicting the former Mayor and indicating that a plaque would not be erected after all), please see the article at page A5 of today's National Post.

Last Friday the Minister of Canadian Heritage, Ms. Sheila Copps, announced that she had officially designated the Gouzenko Affair (1945-1946) as an event of national historic significance. The designation was based on a recommendation by the Historic Sites and Monuments Board of

Canada. A press release and Backgrounder were issued on the Heritage Canada website about this last Friday.

It is conceivable that at some time in the future the federal authorities may seek the City's permission to unveil a federal plaque in Dundonald Park. In such an event I hope the City will grant permission in a timely fashion and not repeat the previous embarrassing mismanagement of the file by taking one year to provide an affirmative answer and then taking another two years to revoke it."

That email was one of the most satisfying I had ever written. My satisfaction was compounded several moments later, when I received two emails. The first was an automatic reply which indicated that the name of Andrea McCormick was not recognized at the City of Ottawa. The second was from Jim Watson at 5:00 p.m. It read:

"Bravo Andrew. I thought of you when I saw the article today. As fate would have it I'm having dinner with Pierre Pagé tonight and will raise it with him. Their suggestion that the Feds wouldn't support this initiative flies in the face of what Ms. Copps has just done! I will work to ensure that the city lives up to its original promise and we'll celebrate together when they have finally come to their senses."

I answered Jim that I was very much looking forward to the celebration with him.

The City Responds

Evidently Mr. Watson did have a chat with the City Clerk about the refusal to move the plaque project forward. At 10:37 p.m. Pierre Pagé, Ottawa City Clerk, sent me an email.

"Thank you for providing me with a copy of your e-mail regarding the unveiling of a plaque. I am replying from home and do not have the file to refer to but as I recall there was no formal approval by the Council of the old City of Ottawa. This matter was forwarded to me for consideration when it was brought to my staff's attention. As you may be aware, staff has been reviewing a significant number of issues since amalgamation including policies, by-laws, etc., from former cities within the RMOC [Regional Municipality of Ottawa-Carleton]. Some of these policies, positions or by-laws have changed or been harmonized. Upon receiving this request, I asked staff to consult with Foreign Affairs as part of the analysis in preparing a response to your request. While Minister Copps may have made the decision to commemorate the event, Foreign Affairs had expressed a serious concern to staff if the City went forward with this commemoration. Specifically, the City was advised that such action could offend the Russian diplomats. On the basis of this advice, I replied that the City would not proceed any further with this commemoration.

I hope this clarifies the position taken on the subject."

I considered his email an invitation to dialogue.

"... While I appreciate receiving your elaboration on the background I already understood the City's position from your letter as well as that of Ms. McCormick in 2001. Your position was already crystal clear to me.

I hope you will agree that few things happen in public that matter without someone or some group of persons being "offended", even if it is just to pretend, as diplomats often do. However, the Cold War has been over for a few years. While I would understand old Stalinists from the Soviet regime wishing to eliminate the Gouzenko Affair from history (and rewrite the history books as they have regularly done to suit their purpose), Russia today is a democratic country. If they are offended by the Gouzenko Affair today it should be because of what their previous government did to us and not because the cipher clerk had courage. The Russians have come a long way towards exposing Stalin's crimes against their own people and distinguishing the former propaganda from the truth. Why is it that this should be a problem in the West?

Similarly, I wonder whether External Affairs thought that the former Soviet regime cared at all about offending the West when they gave Kim Philby a full state funeral in 1988 and gave him the highest designations in the Soviet empire (this was just before the collapse of the Soviet regime). Of course they did not. Did it really make any difference in East/West relations?

While it is true that the former Council did not approve my approval, the Mayor indicated to me in a message to me on receipt of my proposal that he would discuss it with city staff. He subsequently did. Did not one person on the city staff tell him what the process was? While I appreciate that there has since been amalgamation, Ms. McCormick's letter indicated that the former process must be followed until a new one is developed.

When I received a letter from the Mayor, after a year of waiting, indicating that a plaque will be installed and that a person from the city staff has been assigned to the file, I assumed that the proper internal process was being followed. I even specifically asked about that and was assured that all was in order. You cannot imagine my subsequent disappointment to find out several years later from city bureaucrats that the project would be cancelled on the basis of a procedural problem (lack of approval from council) as well as a lack of consultation with federal authorities (was two to three years not enough to figure it out and get it done?)

I made the proposal to the City because a remarkable event that has serious implications for our lives took place in this city and I thought that the City may wish to unveil a plaque to commemorate our heritage and history.

We should be proud of our history and not sweep it under the rug because those who previously wished us ill may be offended that they failed. The unveiling of a plaque does not constitute an "in your face" rubbing of their noses in it. It is merely a dignified way to officially mark a significant event in our history.

Ms. McCormick's rejection letter of 2001 suggested that I apply to the Historic Sites and Monuments Board of Canada, which I did. The federal Historic Sites and Monuments Board of Canada and the Minister of Heritage have done the obvious and made the official designation. I can confirm that the Minister of External Affairs and other Cabinet Minister are in the loop and have been consulted/informed.

Now that I followed the City's advice I merely ask that in the event that the Federal authorities seek permission to place the plaque on City property (i.e., Dundonald Park across from 511 Somerset Street) that the City simply grant permission in a timely fashion. That's all..."

The next morning Mr. Pagé responded:

"I cannot speak for actions which were or were not taken in the past. Unfortunately, while I was responsible for Protocol in the "old" City of Ottawa, this matter was never brought to my attention. I have no background information as to whom former Mayor Watson spoke to in the administration. I will have the matter reviewed once again and get back to you. Within the new City of Ottawa, I am not aware of policies regarding the placement of plaques on City property but will once again review this matter and get back to you."

I forwarded a copy of this exchange of emails to Mr. Watson and thanked him for having discussed the matter with the City Clerk. However, while Mr. Watson appeared hopeful that the City would come around, I had at that time written them off. To me the city had given a whole new meaning to the term dysfunctional. I was still on such a "high" from Sheila Copps' letter and confident that unlike the City, the public announcement which Heritage Canada made was now in the public domain and that Heritage would not renege on their commitment. Indeed, the media was covering it steadily across the country.

The Media Coverage Continues

Supportive newspaper articles and letters to the editor appeared in the *Saskatoon Star Phoenix* (July 23), *Globe and Mail* (July 24), *Windsor Star* (July 24), *Calgary Sun* (July 25), *London Free Press* (July 29). The common theme was that Gouzenko was a man of courage and that this official historic designation was long overdue.

On July 25, the *National Post* printed an article by columnist George Jonas, suggesting that the Heritage Minister's historic designation was an understatement. The article described a party that Svetlana organized in 1995 on the 50th anniversary of her and her late husband's defection. There were many notes and telegrams that arrived, including one that read:

"When you and your husband crossed over to freedom, you began the long process that led to the eventual collapse of the Soviet Union. His revelation helped the West to face up to the reality of communist subversion and tyranny. Those of us who later fought the battle for freedom to its climax in 1989 and 1991 were greatly in his debt – and yours."

The note was signed by Margaret Thatcher.

I sent Evy Wilson an email about the latest articles and noted that the Jonas article revealed that the Gouzenkos had eight children. Accordingly, I wanted to extend warm greetings and words of congratulations to each of them. On July 28, she responded stating that: *"All our large family extend our best wishes to you and your family and send our gratitude for your persistence and determination. We look forward to meeting you in early September."* The September reference was to a public memorial service the family was planning on the first anniversary of the passing of their mother. Evy Wilson had first mentioned this to me the previous year. At the memorial service the family was planning to unveil a headstone with name Gouzenko on it. Thus, the previously unmarked, final resting place of these two heroes would finally become a proudly identified location with the dignity that they deserved. I was looking forward to attending the ceremony and meeting Evy Wilson and other members of her family.

Following-Up with Heritage Canada

The Minister of Heritage had suggested that I call Doug Stewart for more information regarding a plaque unveiling. It took a couple of attempts to reach him, but finally, late in the afternoon of July 26, we spoke. He promised to contact me again in October to start planning the event for the following spring. He further stated that his regional office could only handle four to five ceremonies a year and that this year and next were already fully booked. Accordingly, the ceremony would be held in the Spring, 2004. Their historians would begin working on a plaque text which would be vetted by some expert historians and which Evy Wilson and I would have a chance to comment on. However, there would not be much character space on the plaque itself because of the need for it to be bilingual. In the spring of 2003, they would go back to the HSMBC with a proposed plan which would include the wording of the plaque and the plans for the unveiling ceremony.

More Media Coverage

On July 30, the *Ottawa Citizen* published an interesting article by Chris Champion, titled "The Spy who Helped Us". The article stated that the commemoration was long overdue and ironic because it came from a government that almost sent Gouzenko packing. The article went on to state that the late cipher clerk will be truly vindicated when the small apartment building where he lived is turned into a museum and his critics remembered as dupes. Although I agreed with the contents of the article, I regretted that the title referred to Gouzenko as a spy, because he never was one.

On August 4, the *Washington Times* printed an article by Arnold Beichman, titled "Overdue Recognition for a Cold War Hero". The opening paragraph reads as follows:

"The Canadian government has just honoured - belatedly – a Soviet intelligence agent, Igor Gouzenko, who defected in Ottawa 57 years ago and revealed to the world the existence of a Soviet spy ring in Canada and the United States. Few at the time realized his defection signaled the beginning of the Cold War, Josef Stalin's drive to conquer the Western democracies. Our own government ought to honour the memory of this man, too, because his revelations startled America into a grim realization that the Soviet wartime alliance was over. For good."

I forwarded a copy of the article to Evy Wilson, who replied by email *"Andrew, thank you so much. This "overdue recognition for a Cold War hero" has made my day, my decade! Family members will receive a copy in turn. We extend our utmost thanks to you. Evy"*

The July 30 article in the *Ottawa Citizen* by Chris Champion inspired a lady named Elizabeth Cowan to write a letter to the editor that was published in the *Citizen* on August 7, 2002. The letter reads as follows:

"It was good to see Chris Champion's piece on Igor Gouzenko in the Citizen. The story of this Soviet cipher clerk's defection in 1945 reads like a screenplay for a thriller.

Indeed, Hollywood did film it in 1948, staring Dana Andrews. Among the locations shots was the little apartment building at 511 Somerset St. where the armed NKVD agents smashed down the terrified family's door while they hid with a neighbour. By some stroke of luck, this building has escaped demolition.

Now that the Department of Canadian Heritage has declared the Gouzenko case "an event of national historic significance", could the city not have a plaque placed on the building, as a reminder of those extraordinary times? This was first suggested at least 20 years ago, but better late than never."

I was absolutely thrilled by this outpouring of support in the media and kept forwarding these to the City officials. I was clearly not alone in my fascination with the Gouzenko story and my belief that there should be a historic commemorative plaque. The same morning that Ms. Cowan's letter appeared in the *Ottawa Citizen*, I forwarded the letter electronically to City officials with the following message:

"Further to our previous correspondence on this issue, please see the letter in today's Ottawa Citizen. Although the author suggests a plaque on the building, I believe that a plaque in Dundonald Park across the street from 511 Somerset Street would be more appropriate given that the building is private property and could be torn down someday.

Incidentally, there was another very positive article about the historic designation in a commentary piece in the Washington Times over the past weekend which suggested that a similar designation should be made in the U.S. Who says great ideas don't start north of the border?"

I can only imagine what impact this avalanche of public support for the federal government's decision, the suggestion that it was long overdue, and the suggestion that the City should put up a plaque, had on City officials.

The Public Memorial Service for Igor and Svetlana Gouzenko

On August 30, 2002, I received an email from Evy Wilson saying that the newspaper notices for the memorial service would appear over the next few days in several newspapers. The notice that appeared in the newspapers was a simple yet historic announcement:

"A Memorial Service to Honour Cold War Heroes
Igor and Svetlana Gouzenko
Thursday, September 5, 2002, 4-6 p.m.
Public Welcome
Springcreek Cemetery 1390 Clarkson Road
Mississauga, Ontario"[18]

I arranged to take Thursday and Friday September 5th and 6th off from work, in order to attend the memorial service. On Thursday morning I began the long drive to Evy Wilson's home west of Mississauga, where I had planned to meet her and we would drive to the ceremony together. The weather was perfect and during the long drive I reflected on the struggle of the previous years.

When I arrived at her home we hugged like old friends who had not seen each other in years. The household was hectic, as family members and friends were coming in from out of town to help prepare and attend the ceremony. One of her sisters, Alexandria Boire, arrived from out of town and immediately, upon entering the home, saw me and asked "Who's this?" in a

---

[18] *Globe and Mail*, Saturday, August 31, 2002.

somewhat disturbed tone. When she was informed that I was Andrew Kavchak, the person who pursued the federal historic designation, she immediately smiled and opened her arms to embrace me and express her gratitude for all the work that I had done to make the historic designation possible. Similarly, it was a thrill to meet other family members who were present.

At the cemetery I saw the gravesite and the beautiful headstone with the name Gouzenko on it. A crowd was gathering and a table was set out beside the microphone stand with a display of Gouzenko mementos, such as paintings and books. The family made the necessary preparations to make the memorial service truly special event. Heritage Canada had been contacted and two members of their staff attended the service with Senator Laurier LaPierre. They issued a News Release and Backgrounder for the occasion. A CBC national television reporter was there to cover the event.

The program for the event began with the singing of the national anthem, followed by a prayer of dedication. Then there were a series of speakers. The Master of Ceremonies was one of the Gouzenko sons-in-law. He did a fantastic job. The first speaker was *National Post* columnist, George Jonas, who read a letter from Lord Conrad Black, a family friend, whose letter was just perfect for the occasion. It captured the significance of the Gouzenko saga and the meaning of the ceremony so well. Next, a CSIS employee provided a historical review, while veteran journalist Peter Worthington followed with a memorial tribute to the Gouzenkos. Then Senator Laurier LaPierre gave an address on behalf of the Government of Canada. Finally, Evy Wilson spoke and for the first time publicly identified herself as Evy Gouzenko. It was truly a historic moment which was captured by the television camera. The party then walked over to the gravesite and unveiled the headstone's new plaque. Following the closing remarks there was a reception. There were many cheers and tears. It was an emotional event and I was so happy to have been part of it. At the ceremony I met a number of

Gouzenko family friends and it was a pleasure to shake hands with so many distinguished people.

The timing of the Minister's historic designation, just two months prior was perfect, as it provided a supplementary reason for Heritage Canada to participate in this ceremony. I suspect it also gave the family members the added confidence in knowing that, after all these years, the time was now ripe for them to be able to publicly celebrate and honour their parents.

At the end of the ceremony I approached the two ladies from Heritage Canada, Keri Metcalfe and Dena Rozon, to ask them about the next steps with regard to the plaque commemorating the Gouzenko Affair. They informed me that the next step was to determine the location of the plaque. This was clearly a different first step than was Mr. Stewart told me in July, which was to develop the plaque wording.

After the ceremony the family members and close friends went to a restaurant in Mississauga. We all sat around a very long table and I was fortunate enough to sit across from Evy Wilson. After the dinner I circulated to chat with other people and was informed by the CSIS employee, who spoke at the memorial service, that the Camp X Historical Society had written to Sheila Copps, suggesting that the location of the plaque should be at the site of the former Camp X in Whitby, Ontario. This was the first time that I heard that there was now a competing submission to the HSMBC, with respect to the plaque location. This initially surprised me. Although I suggested to the HSMBC that the plaque be unveiled in Dundonald Park, I was prepared to agree to whatever site Ms. Wilson and the Gouzenko family preferred. I knew Evy Wilson preferred the Department of Justice building on Wellington Street in Ottawa. If that and Dundonald Park were not acceptable then it seemed to me that the Gouzenko gravesite was more appropriate than Whitby. However, we would see how the bureaucrats sorted it out.

After the dinner I returned to Ms. Wilson's home with several family members and friends from out of town, who were going to stay overnight. We said a few toasts and settled around the television to watch the CBC national news, which carried a beautiful report about the ceremony.

The next morning Evy and I had breakfast and chatted some more about the family history. She showed me some of the documents, part of the family archives, which she was sorting through, with a view to contributing to the National Archives. Shortly thereafter, we said our goodbyes and I left for my long drive back to Ottawa.

Following-Up with the City

On September 9, 2002, I sent an email to Pierre Pagé about the memorial service and media coverage. Two days later I received his reply stating:

"I met with the Chief of Protocol yesterday and we are reviewing our decision based on the action of the Federal government. As soon as the review has taken place, I or the Chief of Protocol will be in touch."

On September 11, I sent Jim Watson an updating email about the September 5 ceremony and Pierre Pagé's message that they are reviewing their position. Mr. Watson replied *"...I think the city will come to its senses. I know the media is interested in this story if the city continues to dig in its heels. Keep me posted."*

The next day Tara Peel sent an email to Pierre Pagé, asking that he inform Councillor Arnold of the result once the review was completed. At this point I began to have a change of heart. Whereas previously I did not think seriously that the City would reverse its decision, As Mayor Watson had suggested, the fact that this review was taking some time and that Councillor

Arnold's office was continuing to be interested, suggested that there was some hope. Accordingly, after seeing Ms. Peel's message I sent her office an email stating *"...I am gratified that Mr. Pagé has seen it fit to review the previous unsupportable position and I sincerely hope that the City will unveil a plaque in Dundonald Park to commemorate the events that took place in Ottawa and that had such a pronounced impact on Ottawa and the world."*

Evy Wilson's Media Interview

On Saturday, September 14, the *Globe and Mail* published a half page article based on an interview with Evelyn Wilson. It also included a photo of her in her living room. Ms. Wilson agreed to speak about her previously secret life. The article was a fascinating one, which revealed several remarkable tidbits of information about a truly unusual life. For example, she revealed that her parents had told the children that they were Czech immigrants and that her father was a mining engineer. It was not until Evy was sixteen that she found out that they were not Czech and her father was not a mining engineer, nor had they immigrated here. The four men living downstairs were not boarders, but RCMP agents. She had not been born in Toronto, but a top-secret military location called Camp X. The entire story of their life, their identity and their history, even their names, was invented by the federal government in the 1940s. The Gouzenkos had eight children, and when each found out they rebelled. They wanted to distance themselves from the matter and wished they could be more like their neighbours.

Stalin's Cruelty Continues to be Exposed… in Russia

On September 24, the *National Post* published an article titled "Bones point to Stalin-era mass grave: victims of great terror: Witnesses tell of shots, black vans at army rifle range". The article was about a group of Russian human rights volunteers, known as "Memorial", who had unearthed what they believed to be a mass grave for 30,000 victims of Stalin's "Great

Terror", northwest of St. Petersburg. The article described how the Memorial activists had taken advantage of Russia's new political climate to actively search for leads, documentation and evidence and advertise in local newspapers for eyewitnesses to come forward, to tell what they knew about Stalin's crimes and "to chronicle Stalin's systematic communist terror".

The article described how the residents of a small town called Tosovo, a St. Petersburg suburb, began to tell Memorial investigators of the dark secrets they had witnessed decades earlier. They told of secret police vehicles, black vans, which regularly arrived at the nearby army rifle range in the middle of the night throughout the Great Terror. The vans would stop in the woods, with their engines running and their lights on, before random shots rang out. Apparently the NKVD secret police hoped their executions, of so-called "enemies of the people", would be camouflaged by the regular army exercises which took place on the nearby artillery and rifle ranges. But now volunteers, searching the marshy forests, began to find evidence of summary executions, including skulls shattered by bullet holes, which exactly match those which would have been left by the pistols issued to Stalin's NKVD officers. The article went on to provide more details of what Memorial had discovered about the disappearance of huge numbers of people and the mass murder techniques of the NKVD, including the appearance that the bodies were treated with chemicals to speed their decay.

As soon as I read the article I composed and sent an email to Pierre Pagé.

"Further to your, and the Chief of Protocol's review of your previous decision of last June not to proceed with former Mayor Watson's written commitment to unveil a plaque to commemorate the Gouzenko Affair on the basis that some External Affairs officers in Moscow suggested that it would upset the Russians, please see the article below which appears in today's National Post. Please add this to your file and please consider it when

weighing and reconsidering the "advice" you received from External Affairs in light of Heritage Canada's official historic designation.

Since the days of Gorbachev's "glasnost" the Russians have been researching, exposing and continuously coming to terms with the horrible crimes committed by Stalin, including the murder of millions of their own citizens who were guilty of nothing. These crimes were extensive, and continue to be unearthed. The fact that the KGB was running a spy ring in the West would come today as no surprise to anyone in Russia. The defection of one cipher clerk in Canada to warn the Canadians about the threat to Canadian sovereignty and national security is probably very small potatoes today for the overwhelming majority in Russia (since practically every Russian family was directly affected during Stalin's purges as the article illustrates). As the article demonstrates, the Russian authorities clearly have greater matters of historical nature to deal with and to be upset about.

In other words, the feedback which you received from External Affairs was regrettable because it suggests that we should cover-up the crimes of Stalin and not commemorate an event that helped Canada protect its integrity. I would like to respectfully submit that to suggest that we should forget such significant historical events at a time when the Russians themselves are seeking the truth of their history is inappropriate.

Thank you again for your consideration of this matter. I hope your eventual reassessment of this file will ultimately result in the placing of the city plaque in Dundonald Park. I remember two years ago that Sally Coutts in the city's heritage office who had been assigned to this project told me that the plaque was ready. I have been very eager to see it ever since."

Pierre Pagé responded that same day:

"From the City's point of view (protocol) it was not an issue covering anything up but the City must consider all of the information prior to making a decision. In this particular case, without analyzing the reasons why a particular Embassy may object to a propose course of action, we were advised that the Russian Embassy was going to be offended by the City action. We rely heavily on External Affairs regarding international issues as obviously, the City is not in the business of international relations. In decisions such as this one, we were left with a clear impression that the Government of Canada (through External Affairs) was not endorsing the suggested course of action. Obviously, there appears to be no communication between Heritage and External Affairs as the two departments took opposing views on the matter. I will copy your latest e-mail to the Chief of Protocol and will advise you as soon as a decision is made on this particular issue."

I thanked Mr. Pagé for his reply. However, he had first indicated on July 24, that the matter would be reviewed by the City. Two months later I was still waiting and had no idea when I could expect to hear the result.

At this point I wondered whether I could drum up additional support in the lobbying effort, and contacted Elizabeth Cowen, who had written the August 7 letter in the *Ottawa Citizen*. I thanked her for her letter and gave her the background of my proposal and lobbying effort. I told her that the City was reviewing its position and that any letter she could send to the City in support of a plaque would most likely be helpful in the cause. She agreed to write one and I was grateful for her contribution.

Camp X Authorities Cause a Delay

On October 18, 2002, I sent Michel Audy an email asking if he could tell me of any recent developments and what was happening with respect to the plaque location. Mr. Audy replied on October 23.

"... The Board's decision was to erect the plaque in Dundonald Park. However, Ms. Wilson had suggested installing the plaque at the Justice Building in Ottawa, and the Camp X authorities have made a formal request to receive the plaque on their property.

When the Board reviewed the national historic importance of the Gouzenko Affair, it also considered plaque locations including all of the above. I have explained this to Ms. Wilson and she now supports the Dundonald Park location. In light of the Camp X request however, we are nonetheless asking the Board to reaffirm that Dundonald Park is indeed the place for the plaque, and will do so at its meeting this December. Meanwhile, we will commence work on drafting a plaque text and will involve yourself and Ms. Wilson in any text reviews."

News that the "Camp X authorities" had forwarded their own proposal to the HSMBC about the plaque location, and that it was going to cause a delay, annoyed me considerably. I hoped that the location issue could be settled promptly. Now it was going to have to wait for the next semi-annual Board meeting. In the meantime, I suspected, nothing would be done on the file to move it forward. After all these years of lobbying and waiting, these "authorities" who came out of nowhere were not only holding everything up, but actually threatening to take the plaque to another location, several hours drive away. Within 50 minutes of receiving Mr. Audy's email I responded.

"Thank you for your email and for your ongoing efforts in this regard. With respect to the proposal from "the Camp X authorities" to place the plaque at Camp X, I was surprised when I first heard about their proposal in September at the memorial service which was organized by Ms. Wilson in Mississauga. I very much regret that they made their proposal for several reasons.

First, it is obviously causing delay, diverting energy to review a previously resolved matter, and risks jeopardizing my original proposal of locating the plaque in Dundonald Park.

Second, the location is far out of the way and will likely only be seen by a few people. The large population and tourist centres are in Ottawa, Toronto and Montreal. Camp X is too far removed. Very few people are likely to specifically make a trip to go there and see the plaque. Certainly not more than once. Obviously if the plaque is placed in Dundonald Park in downtown Ottawa it will likely generate much more attention and have a greater impact for years to come.

Third, from a historical point of view, the great drama occurred in Ottawa, not Camp X.

Fourth, if the "Camp X authorities" wanted a plaque about Gouzenko at their location they could have filed an application with the Historic Sites and Monuments Board at any time in the past several decades. To my knowledge, they did no such thing. Instead, this strikes me as a case of "Johnny-come-lately" trying to piggy-back and hijack someone else's project and initiative to achieve a separate objective of promoting Camp X. Frankly, the more I think about it the more I regret their meddling in this matter. While I acknowledge that Camp X played an important part in the history of Canada and that it deserves appropriate recognition, this is not the best way to achieve that objective because it would guarantee that the Gouzenko plaque would be seen by fewer people than would otherwise be the case. I wish the "Camp X authorities" best of luck in pursuing other projects to achieve their objectives (nothing precludes them from making their own separate applications or erecting their own plaques).

Of course, what is most important is that the designation be made and the plaque erected. I am very happy that Minister Copps has made the designation and that the Board already considered several sites for the plaque (including Camp X) and supported my original application suggestion that it be in Dundonald Park. I can assure you that I will attend the unveiling ceremony wherever it will be held, however, I believe that Ottawa is clearly the superior location and I hope that the Board will reaffirm its previous decision to place the plaque in Dundonald Park.

Since I am the individual who originally made the application in 1999 to designate the Gouzenko Affair as a historic event, would you please be so kind as to bring my thoughts on this matter to the attention of the Board when they reconsider this issue at their next meeting (as well as anyone else who may be involved in decision-making about this project)."

Less than ten minutes after sending my email, Mr. Audy replied, thanking me for my comments and confirming that he would inform the Board of my views on the matter. I was confident that my proposal would succeed, but this project was full of the unexpected.

Who is in Charge at City Hall?

Several weeks later, on November 1, 2002, I sent the following email to Mr. Pagé:

"Could you please tell me how are things coming along in the review of your previous decision and whether you have any idea at this point as to when I may expect to receive some (hopefully good) news?"

Tara Peel also emailed Pierre Pagé on the same day asking him to provide Councillor Arnold with an update. When no reply was forthcoming I contacted Ms. Peel on November 7, 2002, to ask if Mr. Pagé had been in touch, and whether they had knowledge about the status of the review.

Within hours Ms. Peel forwarded my email to Mr. Pagé and asked him if he had an update. Weeks passed by with no response.

On December 3, I wrote Councillor Arnold's office the following email:

"I have not heard anything on this file in a long time. As Mr. Pagé's email at the bottom suggests, several months ago the bureaucrats who decided to veto and overrule the Mayor's previous decision regarding the installation of a plaque confirmed that they were going to review their previous decision and get in touch with me. So far nothing has happened and they have not even replied to my previous emails asking about the status. Given that it is unlikely anything will happen over the Christmas and New Year's holiday period, would it be too much to expect that someone could inform me about the status of the review and approximately when the conclusion may be reached? I would very much appreciate a reply in the first half of December (2002) if possible"

Tara Peel forwarded my email to Pierre Pagé (copied to me) and requested: *"Could you please follow-up with Mr. Gouzenko to advise him as to how the City intends to proceed on this?"*

While I would have been deeply honoured and proud if my family name was indeed Gouzenko, this slip of the tongue (or keypad) was too much. I was thoroughly fed up with the treatment I and this file had received. I responded with an email to both Councillor Arnold's office and Pierre Pagé with the following message:

"Just a correction to your email: my name is not Mr. Gouzenko. Mr. Igor Gouzenko died in 1982. I have no relation to the Gouzenko family or name at all. I only made the application in 1999 because the historical commemoration of what Mr. Gouzenko did was long overdue and as an

ordinary Canadian who appreciated the sacrifice he made for our freedom I felt it was a duty. Regrettably, a sentiment not universally shared."

About twenty minutes later Tara Peel apologized for her error. Although I appreciated her message, it still left the main issue with respect to the status of the review unresolved. Accordingly, I followed up with another message:

"… could you please tell me, because I am frankly having difficulty understanding the process, who is in charge at City Hall? I'm not kidding and honestly asking.

I was under the impression that the municipality operated on a democratic basis where citizens (coincidentally also the taxpayers) occasionally got to vote for a representative to the Council. I thought the elected representatives of the people had some authority with respect to the bureaucracy (e.g. the ability to task the people they hire with certain functions).

As this matter drags on from one year to the next, (we are, after all, rapidly approaching 2003), I get the distinct impression that the bureaucrat employees do as they please and ignore repeated requests from you (as well as me). Given that we are the ones who supply their paycheques and that your boss is my elected representative this is a remarkable situation. As it probably occurs on more than just my application I am frankly surprised it is tolerated. Honestly, I would prefer it if Ms. Arnold took a more active role in this matter to bring the erection of the plaque to a conclusion so we can enjoy it instead of talking about it.

Can the elected representatives not ask the bureaucrats to complete whatever it is they are doing within a reasonable time or at least to report on its status. As I look over the history of this file it just leaves me at a loss to explain who is in charge at City Hall"? (Obviously not the Mayor.)

Of course, I don't assume that if their decision is again confirmation of their previous negative decision that that would be the end of the story. But we can cross that bridge if and when we get to it."

This email went unanswered. In the days that followed I became increasingly upset about the City's foot dragging on this issue. How long does it take to review a decision? I suspected that the foot dragging now was primarily because they were seeking another way to wiggle out of the project.

On December 16, I emailed Michel Audy to inquire about the decision of the HSMBC, regarding the plaque location, at their last meeting. No reply was forthcoming.

Time to Let the Media Know

While previously I had wished to keep this project an y difficulties out of the media, for fear of it backfiring and causing more problems, I had now changed my mind. After all the wonderful media coverage in July and September I decided, that if Evy Wilson was prepared to identify herself in public, then there should be no problem with my going public. Accordingly, I decided to take Mr. Watson up on his offer to suggest journalists who might be interested in this story. My primary objective was to get the full story out, so that the public would know just how shameful and unproductive City Hall was on this issue.

Before I could contact Mr. Watson, I received some interesting news from him. After two years as Chief Executive, he announced he would be resigning from the CTC. I received an invitation to his farewell party, to be held on December 20, 2002, at the Fairmont Chateau Laurier. Mr. Watson's new career was going to be as a local media personality, co-host of a noon news show on the local New RO television station in Ottawa.

On December 16, I sent an email to Jim Watson which read:

"... I would like to follow-up on our previous exchanges regarding the City's review of their previous horrible decision to veto your decision about erecting the Gouzenko plaque. As you may recall, I received an email from Mr. Pierre Pagé in September indicating that based on the Heritage Canada decision he met with the Chief of Protocol at the City and that the Chief of Protocol would review the decision and either he or Mr. Pagé would get back to me. In the past month I have sent emails to both Mr. Pagé and Councillor Arnorld's office asking what is the state of the review and when may I expect a response. I have not received any reply and am very disappointed...

In a previous email you suggested that if nothing happens that you know some journalists who would be interested in doing a story on this matter. I am increasingly tempted to tell the story. Right now I feel that if I do not get a meaningful response by the end of this month that I would be prepared to pursue a media story in January. Would you have any advice or references to the journalists that you were thinking of who might be interested?

I did not have long to wait. Two days later Mr. Watson, replied:

"Hi Andrew- thanks for the update. I will be starting a new column with the Citizen in addition my TV show in January, and I want to feature your struggle as one of the first stories. Can you send me a copy of everything you have to date and then I will call you to set up a time to speak to you and see if we can finally get this very good idea off the ground. Keep the faith! Thanks. You can send copies of material to me.... – the sooner I get it the better. Thanks!"

Fantastic! Clicking with the media could not have been easier. I could not believe my good fortune. The former Mayor who had approved my proposal, which was then vetoed by some bureaucrats, was now going to be in a position to write about it in the city newspaper. I spent the next two days reviewing my files and selecting the most relevant documents for photocopying. I also prepared a chronology of events outlining the highlights of the various stages that this project had gone through. On December 20, I arrived at his farewell party during the speeches and gift presentations. Afterwards I exchanged a few words with Mr. Watson. His new column in the *Ottawa Citizen* was going to be a weekly column and the staff at the *Citizen* had expressed that they wanted the Gouzenko story to be the subject of his first column. He indicated that he would like me to appear on his television program as well. I informed him that I was preparing a package of background documents, which I dropped off at his home the following morning.

CHAPTER 6: 2003 – A REVERSAL OF FORTUNE

Communication with Evy Wilson

On January 2, 2003, I informed Evy Wilson of Jim Watson's first article in the *Citizen* was slated for Monday, January 13, and that the story would also be covered at noon on his TV news show. She responded a few hours later with the following message:

"It's such a joy to receive your messages. You are a very positive person with persistence and determination – key ingredients for success in any endeavor. Your participation in our political drama is truly God sent, bringing forth an amazing turnaround in public awareness and opinion. Not easy feats. I am so pleased and uplifted by your decision and courage to be publicly connected to our story. You are an excellent spokesperson... At some point, I may wish to talk about the relief... and apprehension... of public disclosure of our true identify. Anyone directly or indirectly connected to the secret world of espionage and intelligence has second thoughts. Yet, the value of the truth is worth the risk."

The HSMBC Confirms the Plaque Location

On January 6, 2003, I sent Michel Audy an email following-up on my previous message of December 16, 2002, asking whether the HSMBC had confirmed a location for the plaque. I suspected he had been away on holidays. Later that day I received a reply, apologizing that he had been away from the office for five weeks, due to circumstances beyond his control. His email included the following paragraph:

"Regarding the plaque location for the Gouzenko Affair, the HSMBC reaffirmed its previous recommendation which is Dundonald Park in Ottawa. Parks Canada staff will now be working to finalize plaque text and organize a plaque unveiling ceremony. My office will advise those who proposed alternative plaque locations with these results."

Media Preparation

In early January, I received a phone call from an *Ottawa Citizen* photographer, who asked if we could meet in Dundonald Park, to take pictures of me in front of 511 Somerset Street. We met on January 7, at lunchtime. The conditions were perfect, as it was a sunny morning without a cloud in the sky. Also on January 7, I received a call from Karen Murray, producer of the noon TV news show at the New RO station who wanted to discuss with me the content of what I could say and the format for my appearance. This was a wonderful exercise for me as I had to distill into just a few minutes both the Igor Gouzenko story and the struggle I had over the previous three and half years. However, something happened the next morning which changed the story significantly.

The City Changes its Mind: The Second Commitment

On January 8, Councillor Arnold forwarded an email message that she had received about an hour earlier from Bernadine Clifford, Protocol Officer. Ms. Clifford's message was addressed to someone by the name of Gilles Seguin.

"Following discussions with the City Clerk and Chief of Protocol, could you please proceed with the plans for the installation of a plaque in Dundonald Park. We would like this commemoration to take place in early spring.

Staff in the Office of Protocol would be pleased to work with you and Councillor Arnold's Office to assist with the coordination of a ceremony."

In her covering message, Councillor Elisabeth Arnorld wrote me:

"Please see the attached response that I received from the Office of Protocol here at the City indicating that the City will proceed with the installation of a commemorative plaque in Dundonald Park in the spring. I look forward to seeing this plaque installed to recognize the historical significance of 511 Somerset Street West. My office will be in touch with you as the details about the ceremony are finalized. Thank you for all your work on this issue."

Victory! A new and second commitment from the City of Ottawa! However, it seemed odd that they did not have to run it by Council this time and get its approval, as Ms. McCormick had previously claimed. Since that was the case, I wondered whether it was also necessary to consult with DFAIT. The news did not come to me from the Chief of Protocol or the City Clerk himself, as Mr. Pagé had repeatedly claimed it would. Nonetheless, I was not complaining. I responded within minutes, thanking her for the great news and asking if it would be possible to obtain a formal written commitment. I did not receive a reply. I promptly passed on the news to Evy Wilson. I also forwarded Councillor Arnold's news to Jim Watson by email and called him and Patrick Dare, an editor at the *Ottawa Citizen*, to let them know that the conclusion to Mr. Watson's article, slated for publication the following Monday, January 13, might need to be changed. Mr. Watson suggested only a minor change in the ending. In the meantime I had been contacted by the producer of the New RO new program and was informed that the producers had arranged for Councillor Arnold to be interviewed in Dundonald Park on January 13.

Meanwhile, in England a related historical event took place. Newspaper reports indicated that Alan Nunn May, a British scientist working in Canada during WWII, and the first of the atom bomb spies to be caught, thanks to Igor Gouzenko, had died on January 12, 2003, at the age of 91.

Monday, January 13, 2003 – Front Page News!

Early on Monday, January 13, as soon as I woke up I drove to the nearest *Citizen* newspaper box. It was dark and cold. I figured that the story would be in the "City" section of the newspaper. But as I approached the newspaper box my heart skipped a beat. A colour picture of me, holding the 1946 Royal Commission Report with the building at 511 Somerset Street in the background, was on the front page, above the fold. With the clear blue skies in the background it made a powerful visual impression. The day's front-page headline was about my efforts, and read:

"Our 'Ordinary hero': Fifty-eight years after a Soviet embassy clerk exposed spies in our midst, and after one man's three-year struggle to mark the historic event, the city is finally prepared to honour Igor Gouzenko".

I immediately bought two copies and drove home, anxious to read the article. In all the fuss I had almost forgotten that it was my son Michael's fourth birthday. The article was a lengthy and well-written chronology of my lobbying struggle since 1999. It contained some humour, as well as sadness and sorrow as it reflected on the death of Svetlana Gouzenko. Among other things, the article suggested that the red tape I had encountered was similar to what Gouzenko had experienced.

I called Evy Wilson later that morning and left a message indicating that I would forward the article that morning. She soon replied:

"Overjoyed! Thank you so much for all your wonderful effort... Your message was so appreciated. I've now shared this moment with family members... Good luck at noon today. Hope to talk to you later."

At work I began to receive a number of congratulatory emails and phone calls from friends and acquaintances. Many had known of my efforts, but others were surprised by it all.

Live from Dundonald Park!

From work I walked over to Dundonald Park where I met the interviewer, Karen Solomon and the New RO cameraman. It was a cold day, so we stayed in the heated van containing all the television equipment. Councillor Arnold appeared and we briefly chatted. I thanked her for the news of the previous Wednesday and expressed my sincere appreciation of her efforts over the years. Councillor Arnold and I were interviewed separately. When the time came, the other three conducted a live interview in the middle of the park, which I could hear while I waited in the van. It was a truly satisfying moment to hear Councillor Arnold confirm that the City would be unveiling the plaque in the Spring and that it hoped members of the Gouzenko family could attend. I was subsequently interviewed in two segments and gave an overview of the defection and my lobbying efforts.

The television interview gave me a new sense of success and the feeling that all the headaches of the past few years had been worth it. I had commitments from two levels of government to erect commemorative plaques and the media publicity was getting the story out. The Gouzenko story would be known to a new generation of Canadians.

The feedback which I received from friends and acquaintances was very satisfying. However, the cherry on top is when a stranger makes a public statement about it. That is what happened on January 17, when the *Ottawa Citizen* published a letter from a lady named Irena Bell:

"Jim Watson's first column for the Citizen was terrific. Soviet defector Igor Gouzenko has indeed never been properly recognized for his heroism in 1945. Kudos to Andrew Kavchak for his persistence in battling all odds to get some long-overdue acknowledgment of Mr. Gouzenko's courage and contribution to Canada's freedom."

Following-Up with HSMBC

When Mr. Watson's article came out on January 13, I thought someone from Heritage Canada would call to discuss the article and my lobbying the City and the status of the file. No one did.

On February 3 and 4, I called Doug Stewart at the Rideau Canal Office of Parks Canada and left a message. His secretary explained that he was busy in meetings and that she had not heard anything about the file since the previous July. They were unaware that it had been front page news in Ottawa. On February 5, I received a phone call from Mr. John Grenville of the Kingston office of Parks Canada. My messages to Mr. Stewart were passed on to him as Mr. Grenville now had control of the file, which he had just received. I thought the local office would be in Ottawa, but that was not the case. I tried to get a feeling from him as to what stage the file was at and how much he knew. It turned out that he was not aware of the decision of the HSMBC from December regarding the location.

Mr. Grenville stated that the next steps involved requesting a draft text for the plaque, which would be most likely prepared by the historian who worked on the application, Catherine Cournoyer. The plaque itself would be the standard 27" by 30" size with bilingual text and would contain only 600 characters for explaining the importance to the nation. The historian should get a draft ready by July, 2003. Mr. Grenville would then have about six weeks to get it out for comments. He would then get the feedback and "roll it up". The new draft with comments would go to the inscriptions committee, a sub-committee of the HSMBC. It would then take about 5-6 weeks to get the plaque cast. The unveiling ceremony would be sometime in the Spring of 2004. Although I would have appreciated an earlier date, there was nothing I could do to speed things up.

During the conversation I provided Mr. Grenville with the background concerning my application to the City of Ottawa and told him that the City had now confirmed that they were going to erect a plaque in Dundonald Park in the Spring. I suggested that it might be worthwhile to contact the City of Ottawa in order to coordinate the landscaping and locations of the plaques in the park as well as to be aware of the wording of the separate texts to ensure there is no conflict and no unnecessary repetition so that they would complement each other. I wanted to give him the telephone number of Councillor Arnold at the City so he could find out who was now working on the file, but I did not have the number handy at the time of our conversation. However, while I was describing to him the background I mentioned the name of Sally Coutts and he then said that he knew her and would just send her an email asking her who was working on it now at the City instead of waiting for me to retrieve Councillor Arnold's phone number. I had a feeling that was not going to work, but he seemed confident.

The City Sets a Tentative Date

On February 10 and 12, I had several telephone conversations with Tara Peel. She told me that Bernadine Clifford of the Office of Protocol had the lead on the file and would use the same wording for the plaque as had been previously agreed to in 2000. She would also contact the Mayor's office with respect to timing, most likely to be April or May. There would be an invitation list which would include the officials from the local heritage association and probably people who lived near the site. She promised to contact Ms. Clifford about every ten days for an update.

On February 18, I called Bernadine Clifford to find out how things were progressing and whether I could assist in any way. It was a good thing I did so. She said that nothing had happened on the file as she was still going through it and figuring it out. She had a proposed plaque text, but did not know if it was the final one agreed to in 2000. I asked her to fax it to me so I could verify. She confirmed that she was going to target sometime in May for the ceremony. Ms. Clifford also said that Mayor Bob Chiarelli expressed a desire to have an internal meeting to discuss what he wanted with respect to the ceremony. This was good news. I requested that she confirm the date and time with Evy Wilson and myself as soon as possible, so that we could inform family and friends.

Shortly after my call a fax arrived with the proposed text in English and in French. I recognized the English text from our dealings with Sally Coutts in 2000, but had never seen the French text before. I was glad that the City was proceeding with a bilingual text, but felt that it should have been vetted by myself and the Gouzenko family, just as the English text had been. I forwarded both items by fax to Evy Wilson, who subsequently confirmed that the English text was indeed the third and final version that her mother had seen and agreed to in 2000.

With respect to the French text, however, I immediately noticed that the first paragraph was poorly translated. Accordingly, I asked a friend, whose French was first class, to take a look and comment upon it. I used these as the basis of an email to Bernadine Clifford, sent February 19, in which were identified some poor phrase translations, typographical and grammatical errors and an omission. After bringing there to her attention I suggested that the French text be reviewed again. I hoped the City would revise it and take my comments into account. However, I was never shown a second version.

At this time another related historical event was reported in the media. On March 5, 2003, the world observed the 50th anniversary of the death of Joseph Stalin.

The City Creates Another Committee

On March 7, I sent an update to Evy Wilson.

"… I called Tara Peel in Elisabeth Arnold's office to ask her about what's happening. It turns out that the Mayor, Bob Chiarelli, already had his meeting with Pierre Pagé, Elisabeth Arnold, etc. to discuss this file. Apparently he was concerned that if there is not some formal process that the city may get flooded with commemorative requests and they did not want this to stick out as an anomaly. Accordingly, it will go before a "commemoration naming committee" on Monday. Jesus! Another goddamn committee!! However, Elisabeth Arnold has apparently confirmed that this project is meant to go ahead and that this committee review is a formality. Tara said she would call me next week with an update (that never seems to happen – it's always me who calls)…"

A second update followed on March 11, 2003.

"Good news. I just got a call from Tara Peel, assistant to Councillor Arnold. This is historic in itself as it is one of the few times she has called me with an update.

It appears that the matter was considered yesterday by the commemorative naming committee of the City of Ottawa, composed of 5 bureaucrats from different departments (not politicians). They appear to have considered it rather quickly, rubber stamped it, and now Tara has sent an email to the Protocol office (Bernadine Clifford) indicating that the formal process of approval has been followed and asking the Protocol office to get on with the unveiling ceremony for some time in May.

The next steps are for the Protocol office to finalize the French wording as per my comments of a few weeks ago, to make the plaque, set the date, make the snow melt (there is a lot of it in Ottawa right now), lay the foundation for the plaque, arrange the ceremony, send out invitations to the privileged, etc...

Overall this is good news. Approximately 1,100 days have passed since my first application, and it may be that we have only another 70 to go. Wow."

On March 18, I called Bernadine Clifford who told me that the next steps would be to get the plaque wording finalized and then to propose and confirm a date with Councillor Arnold's office and the Gouzenko family. Six days later, Bernadine Clifford sent Evy Wilson an email stating the following:

"I have been asked to assist in the coordination of the Plaque Commemoration for Igor Gouzenko. Councillor Arnold recommended that the commemoration take place on Saturday, May 3rd, perhaps at 10:00 a.m. Could you please advise if this date and time might be suitable for you and members of your family. Once the date and time has been confirmed, I would appreciate receiving a list of guests that you would like invited to attend.

Andrew has confirmed with me that the wording of the plaque is acceptable to you and members of your family and I have forwarded the document to our translation services for proofing of the French text."

Evy Wilson replied March 25, that her family was honoured by this meaningful event. However she indicated that having the ceremony between June 2nd and 5th would be more convenient for her, as she was planning to attend another event in Ottawa that week. While I regretted the request for a delay, one had to be flexible, due to her coming from out of town. Bernadine Clifford responded the next day to Evy Wilson and Councillor Arnold.

"This is to inform that the Mayor's schedule has tentatively been booked for Wednesday, June 4th from 3:30 p.m. to 5:00 p.m. I will contact you again as soon as I receive confirmation. In the meantime, in anticipation of this event in June, could you please provide me with a list of guests you would like to invite?"

As the tentative date of the ceremony approached I sensed a degree of anxiety developing. A little humour has always helped relive such tension. On March 28, I sent an email to Evy Wilson.

"I was talking with a friend of mine here about the upcoming ceremony and he suggested that there should be a mass distribution to everyone in attendance of commemorative and souvenir pillow cases with the date on it of the unveiling ceremony. Wouldn't that be great?

Also, some people have asked me what project would I be working on after this is all over and responded recently that I may decide to start lobbying the City to rename Charlotte Street to "Gouzenko Avenue". Wouldn't it be hilarious if the Russian Embassy had to notify everyone of their change of address to Gouzenko Boulevard or something. Have a good weekend!"

She responded later that day.

"You have an extraordinary sense of humour. It rivals my father's who Peter Worthington once described as having "dry wit". My dad had a great sense of humour, when you got to know him. He'd probably enjoy the souvenir pillowcase. There would truly be poetic justice in the Charlotte Street's web paying to tribute to his name, a name he could not use for most of his life and his children cannot carry. Are you prepared for the June 4th ceremony? I sensed somewhat high anxiety from the conference organizers who like my lawyer wishes it would just all go away. That always seems to happen whenever there is even a modicum of public honour or justice. So much controversy. Few of us can really take it."

Connecting the HSMBC with the City

On April 8, I sent an email to John Grenville at Heritage Canada following-up on our conversation of February 5, to ask how the project was coming along at his end. I decided to inform him, just in case he had not heard, that the person working on the file at the City of Ottawa was Bernadine Clifford, and provide her contact information. Mr. Grenville emailed his thanks for the information about the City contact. He indicated that he had sent Sally Coutts a message but still did not have a contact name. He confirmed that he wanted to co-ordinate the design for the installation of the federal plaque with the City's and had asked for a draft text for the Gouzenko Affair plaque.

Following-Up with the City

On April 4, I called Bernadine Clifford and learned that she had not yet received confirmation from the Mayor's office about the time and date for the ceremony, but would call to follow-up. She further confirmed that she now had the texts in English and French and that the plaque would be made by a private company and not internally by the City. The next steps were for

Ms. Wilson to forward her lists of people for the City to invite and for the City to confirm the date and time.

On April 14, I called Tara Peel to see if she would give me any information about the status. Ms. Peel thought June 4th was a confirmed date, leaving me wondering whether the Mayor's office had forgotten to inform Ms. Wilson and myself. With respect to other logistical questions, and whether I would be allowed to speak at the ceremony, Ms. Peel had no idea, but responded that the Office of Protocol had experience and would take care of everything. I followed up with Bernadine Clifford on April 23.

"Further to your email below of last month, could you please tell me what is the status of confirmation of the unveiling date for the Gouzenko plaque? I believe that the proposed June 4 date and time is good. As soon as you can confirm the date and time I will notify the family and friends that I know would like to attend the ceremony, however, I would prefer to do it sooner, rather than later, so that we can all make the necessary plans to attend."

I also indicated in the email that I would like an opportunity to say a few words at the ceremony.

From "Tentative" to "Firm": The City Confirms the Date

On April 28, Bernadine Clifford sent an email to Evy Wilson with a copy to me stating:

"Thank you both for your recent email correspondence. I am currently working on 9 different events (yours included) and as you can understand, I must devote some of my time to the events that will take place in April and May.

I must say that I was discouraged last week when I asked for an update on the design of the plaque and was informed that nothing had been done on it during the past month! However, I hope to have a proof of the design this week. Likewise, I hope to have a proof of the bilingual invitation this week.

I have received confirmation that the Mayor will attend the ceremony on Wednesday, June 4th at 3:30 p.m. in Dundonald Park. I believe the ceremony itself will take about 20 to 30 minutes, followed by a small reception.

... I will be working on the Itinerary for the event soon and will take into consideration your request to make brief comments. Thank you for your patience..."

This email brought both good and bad news. The good news was that we had confirmation of a ceremony date and time, as well as the Mayor's presence. The bad news was that another month had gone by with no progress on the development of the plaque. This was very puzzling as I had previously been told that the plaque was ready by several different people at various times. Although I was given the opportunity to submit a guest list for the City to send invitations to, I did not act on it. It was clear that Ms. Clifford had enough work and things were not moving fast on this file. I would issue invitations to my family and friends myself.

Following-Up with the HSMBC

That same day, I called Michel Audy to inform him of the date of the City's plaque unveiling ceremony and invited him to attend. To my surprise he did not know about the *Citizen* article. Furthermore, although City of Ottawa officials had called to inquire about the Minister's historic designation, he was unaware of any initiative with the City. I also emailed John Grenville the date, time and location of the City's plaque unveiling ceremony and expressed the hope that he would be able to attend. He responded that it was on his calendar and he would try to be there.

Jim Watson Gets Back into Politics

During the week of April 28, Jim Watson announced that he was taking a leave of absence from journalism and would seek the liberal nomination in the provincial riding of Ottawa West/Nepean. I sincerely hoped that he would win, although I regretted that he would no longer be able to direct any media coverage to the unveiling ceremony.

The City Sends out the Invitations – No Turning Back Now

On May 7 and 9, I called Ms. Clifford to inquire about the City's invitation cards. The invitation cared was faxed to me at the end of the day on Friday, May 9. It was a great way to start off the weekend. The invitation card had the City of Ottawa logo on it and beside the heading "Invitation" it read:

"His Worship Bob Chiarelli Mayor of the City of Ottawa and City Councillor Elisabeth Arnold, Somerset Ward request the pleasure of your company at a Plaque Unveiling Ceremony to commemorate Igor and Svetlana Gouzenko in recognition of their historic flight to freedom in 1945, Wednesday, June 4, 2003, 3:30 p.m. Dundonald Park, Ottawa 516 Somerset Street West (corner of Somerset and Lyon) Business Attire, Reception to follow R.S.V.P."

The invitation card provided the telephone number of the City's Office of Protocol so that they would have an idea of how many people were coming. This was a major milestone. In less than a month my dream from 1999 was about to come true.

CHAPTER 7: THE CEREMONY OF JUNE 4, 2003 AND ITS MEANING

Advance Media Publicity

In order to generate publicity and media coverage, I contacted a few journalists in late May to let them know about the upcoming ceremony. On May 27, I had a telephone interview with Jeff Sallot of the *Globe and Mail*. On Saturday, May 31, the *Globe* ran his article titled "Remembering Soviet Defector Igor Gouzenko", which included a colour picture of me in front of 511 Somerset Street and a picture of Gouzenko. The article reported that I had lobbied for a plaque for years and that one was finally going to be unveiled the following Wednesday. It contained a couple of quotes from our interview, including my comment that we appear to have a difficult time dealing with the concept of heroes in Canada. Gouzenko's importance was also highlighted with quotes from Professor Martin Rudner of Carleton University and from *The Mitrokhin Archive*. The article created a multiplier effect.

On Monday, June 2, Holly Lake, of the *Ottawa Sun*, interviewed me for a story that ran the next day. Also, on June 2, CBC radio called asking me to come to their studios the next day, to tape an interview with the host of the "All in a Day" program, Brent Bambury.

Tuesday, June 3, 2003

On the morning of June 3, I went to the CBC radio studios, on the top floor of the Fairmont Chateau Laurier hotel. The interview went well and was aired that afternoon. After the taping, the CBC producers asked me to walk over to another studio, to do a similar interview with a host in Toronto. Bernard St-Laurent was filling in for Shelagh Rogers and the interview was broadcast the following morning on the national CBC radio program "Sounds Like Canada".

Upon returning to the office, I received a call from the New RO television station, asking if I could be in the studio at noon, on June 4, for a live interview. Another call came from a CBC Newsworld producer in Toronto, who wanted to know if I could do a live national television interview the following morning. After so many years of lobbying in the wilderness, the story was finally going to become known publicly.

At lunchtime, I walked to the park to check out the plaque installation. While the pedestal was installed, there was no panel on top of it. I called Bernadine Clifford to inquire as to the status. She said that the plaque was being manufactured out of town. Though late, it was on its way and would arrive in Ottawa during the morning of June 4. It would be installed by noon, if everything went according to plan. What if things did not go according to plan? I did not dare to think about it.

June 4, 2003 – An Unforgettable Day

I looked at the clock on the bedside table and it was 2:30 a.m. In just a few hours I would have to go downtown for a live national television interview with Alison Smith on CBC Newsworld. This was a dream come true, but I was so excited I was having difficulty sleeping. Somehow I managed to doze off into a light sleep. Eventually the alarm went off, instantly waking me. "This is it!" I thought to myself. After four years of lobbying the City of Ottawa to unveil a commemorative plaque honouring one of the greatest heroes in our country's history, finally today was the day. And it was going to be a full day, like nothing I had experienced since my wedding five years earlier. The plaque unveiling ceremony was scheduled to start at 3:30 p.m. in Dundonald Park, but first I had two live television appearances to make. The first would be on national TV, and the second on a local independent television station at noon.

I quickly had coffee and breakfast and said goodbye to my wife Sylvie and our two children. I was told that for the 7:45 a.m. part of the show I had to show up by 7:15 a.m. I got there early, and I am glad I did. There was no one on the roads at that that time and finding a parking spot was no problem.

At the park I met two CBC technicians who were setting up their equipment. The cameraman was the chief and the other was his assistant. The camera was set up so that the building at 511 Somerset Street, across the street, was in the background. After relating this story to individuals on a one to one basis for four years, I was about to address a national audience. The cameraman asked me a few questions, then told me that my answers were much too long and would have to be dramatically shortened.

I stood next to where the plaque was to be installed. The bare pedestal was there, and I hoped that the plaque would be installed around noon as I had been informed. The microphone and ear plug were adjusted and fitted on me. I could hear the broadcast as it was running. Business news, followed by weather and sports. Then a commercial break. Alison Smith then said into the microphone "Hello Mr. Kavchak, it's Alison Smith, can you hear me?"

The weather was sunny and it was warming up. However, there were so many trees that I was in the shade. Additional bright lights were necessary, which made me feel like I was staring at the sun. My heart was beating rapidly in anticipation of getting this story out. Countdown… end of commercial. And then Alison Smith gave her introduction.

"A man who came to be known as Canada's cold war hero is being honoured today in Ottawa. On September the fifth, 1945, Igor Gouzenko defected from the Soviet Embassy bringing with him details of a communist spy rink in Canada. He was granted political asylum but remained in hiding for the rest of his life, often appearing in public with a bag over his head. Today Gouzenko's bravery will be formally recognized when a plaque is unveiled in Ottawa. Andrew Kavchak has been lobbying for years to get the City to honour Gouzenko. He will be part of today's ceremony and he joins me now from Dundonald Park in Ottawa where the plaque is going to be unveiled. Mr. Kavchak, tell me why Mr. Gouzenko is so important to you…"

"Showtime!" I thought to myself. The interview provided me with a chance to recount the drama of the defection and respond to several questions including whether there was any resistance to my application. I was quite satisfied and relieved when it was over. The first challenge of the day had gone well.

Returning home, I received calls from Adam Grachnik of the *Ottawa Citizen* and Steven Fisher of CBC Ottawa TV. I told them I would be in the park before the ceremony and would be available there for interviews. Then I was off to the New RO television studios for a live interview at noon with guest host Alex Munter, Deputy Mayor of the City of Ottawa. The interview went well, after which I returned to the park. To my relief the plaque had been delivered and installed. It was beautiful. I met Bernadine Clifford and then gave several media interviews, including one with Joy Malbon of CTV. William Kelly, former Deputy Commissioner of the RCMP, dropped by before the ceremony and I had my picture taken with him beside the plaque.

A large crowd gathered before the ceremony. I hugged Evy Wilson and her sister Alexandria Boire when they arrived. Several other Gouzenko family members, including grandchildren, were present, as well as my own family and friends. There were also many persons I did not know. It was brought to my attention that the *Ottawa Citizen* had carried an editorial that day, titled "Remember Gouzenko", while the *Ottawa Sun* had awarded me their "Thumbs Up" award on the editorial page.

Just before the ceremony began, as Evy Wilson and I were getting ready, a well-dressed and very polite gentleman approached. He asked if I was Andrew Kavchak and pulled out a faxed letter that I had sent to the American Ambassador, Paul Cellucci, inviting him to attend the ceremony. My letter suggested that it would be an honour to have our great ally represented at this event. If he could not attend, I hoped he would send a representative. The gentleman asked if I had written the letter. When I told him that I had, he confirmed that he was there from the U.S. Embassy. We shook hands and I thanked him for joining us.

The Ceremony

The Master of Ceremonies was Councillor Arnold. There were four speakers: the Mayor, followed by Councillor Arnold, Evy Wilson, and myself. In his speech the Mayor stated that after 9-11 and the start of a new war on terrorism, it was useful to recognize and remember the Gouzenko Affair and the call to arms against the totalitarian communism of Stalin's Soviet Union. He recounted the story of the Gouzenko defection and stated that:

"We shudder to think of the ramifications, had the Gouzenkos not defected to Canada and revealed the Soviet espionage networks that were operating in Canada and other countries. Igor Gouzenko accomplished an historical and heroic act when he defected to Canada... This selfless act cost

him the loss of his identify, and that of his family. But it gave to Canada and the world democracies a wake-up call to protect and defend themselves against the dangers of 'The Cold War'".

He concluded by quoting the Royal Commission's statement that Gouzenko had rendered a great public service to the people of this country and placed Canada in his debt. The Mayor went on to say that the entire free world was in his debt and today Ottawa, and Canada, were saying thank you. It was an excellent speech. Councillor Arnold's and Evy Wilson's were also special. Ms. Wilson was particularly dramatic when she held up and showed her parents' citizenship papers, signed by King George VI. After thanking those who made the plaque possible, she went on to state:

"Over half a century ago, our parents Svetlana and Igor Gouzenko escaped Soviet tyranny into the arms of freedom – here, in Ottawa, Canada. Their brave decision has made this day possible. Their dire warning was heeded.

Dundonald Park provided the backdrop for this unfolding drama that still continues today. Thus, the City of Ottawa commemorative plaque is a fitting tribute, a gift of historic insight and memorial, not only for my parents and all Canadians but also for the free Russian people today and for those who perished, that their memory not be forgotten.

It is a reminder that we must never take for granted our freedoms and liberties.

In 1947, by this document [Citizenship Indenture displayed] and under the 'Great Seal of Canada', King George VI bestowed citizenship upon my father, mother, young brother and me. Our parents considered this privilege, this freedom, their greatest reward.

Three months after their escape, I was born while our parents and their young son were held in protective custody at Camp X near Oshawa. As their eldest daughter and the chosen family representative, in gratitude for this great honour, I know that I speak for my large family and from the heart when I say: thank you, Je vous remercie, spasiba."

When it was my turn to speak at the podium I did not need the notes, folded in my pocket, as I knew exactly what I wanted to say. After thanking all the people at City Hall who helped make this possible, I specifically thanked former Mayor Jim Watson, Mayor Bob Chiarelli, Councillor Arnold, Tara Peel, and Bernadine Clifford. Thanking my wife for her support and patience over the years, I went on to say:

"Today is truly a very special day. And to me, I can only describe it as a dream come true. In 1999 I had moved to this neighbourhood and visited this park on a daily basis with my son. I could not believe that there was no mark here to let visitors know of the truly remarkable events that took place here in September, 1945. So I decided to start lobbying the municipal and federal governments to mark the historic significance of this location with the erection of commemorative plaques. And here we are, 1,395 days later, and we are finally unveiling a historic plaque. This is truly a dream come true.

I believe that every individual and every nation should have a hero. Heroes serve an important function and role in society. When non-negotiable principles and values are threated, heroes show us what can be done to protect them. Heroes don't just talk about it, but they actually do it, often, a great personal risk and sacrifice. Thus, heroes motivate and inspire. I am proud to say that Igor and Svetlana Gouzenko are my heroes.

When I first started my application process I knew that Igor Gouzenko had died in 1982. However, I did not know if Svetlana Gouzenko was still alive. I subsequently found out in my research that she was and hoped that she would have been able to attend this ceremony, which was originally scheduled for the year 2000, and witness this tribute to a living legend. I also hoped to meet her in person, so I could tell her something that I have wanted to tell her for a long time.

Unfortunately, this ceremony was postponed due to factors beyond my control and Svetlana Gouzenko passed away in September 2001. It was a sad time. However, her soul and that of her husband are witnessing this event from the heavens above, their spirits are all around, and in the company of some of their descendants I would like to say:

Dear Mr. and Mrs. Gouzenko...On behalf of a generation of Canadians born after September 1945 into a country blessed with freedom, a freedom that you did so much to protect and preserve, I say: 'Thank you! Thank you! Thank you!'

This plaque will mean different things to different people, but to me it means that the residents of Ottawa and Citizens of Canada remember our friends and heroes and take the steps to ensure that future generations will never forget. And just to underscore that, the Federal Heritage Minister, Sheila Copps, sent me a letter last July indicating that on the positive recommendation of the Historic Sites and Monuments Board of Canada, she had designated the Gouzenko Affair as an event of national historic significance and committed the Heritage Department ton unveiling a federal plaque in this park next year. And so we will have an opportunity to pay tribute to our heroes again, at another ceremony, in only another 365 days. I hope we will see each other again at that time. Thank you."

The other speakers and I held the black cloth covering the plaque and pulled it back to unveil it as cameras snapped pictures and the crowd burst into applause. The Mayor read the first paragraph in English and Councillor Arnold read the first paragraph in French. The Mayor and I then presented

Evy Wilson with a framed replica of the plaque. The City's official photographer and the media took many pictures of Evy Wilson holding the replica with 511 Somerset Street in the background. History was in the making.

The plaque is a navy blue colour and contains bilingual text, with the name Igor Gouzenko in large print on a gold coloured stripe across the middle, separating the English text on top from the French on the bottom. There are three pictures on the Plaque: the apartment building at 511 Somerset Street; Gouzenko with his famous trademark hood, standing beside the actress who portrayed his wife in the film "Operation Manhunt", and the old Soviet Embassy. The English text on the panel reads as follows:

"This panel is erected by the City of Ottawa in recognition of the courage of Igor Gouzenko and his wife Svetlana for their historic flight to freedom in Canada on September 5, 1945.

That night, when Igor Gouzenko left the Soviet Embassy on Charlotte Street in Ottawa, he carried 109 carefully selected documents that proved that the Soviet Union was engaged in espionage against its allies. An historic international event, it was to influence foreign policy in Great Britain, the United States, and many other countries around the globe.

Gouzenko went to the newsroom of the Ottawa Journal to offer the evidence of Soviet espionage in Canada. Unfortunately, staff rejected what would have been the "scoop of the century" and suggested Gouzenko return in the morning or go to the RCMP. Gouzenko then approached the offices of the Minister of Justice, Louis St. Laurent, but was again told to come back in the morning. He returned home late to 511 Somerset Avenue West and spent an anxious night with his expectant wife and infant son.

The next day, September 6, 1945, Gouzneko returned to the offices of the Minister of Justice and to the Ottawa Journal, and was again turned away. Gouzenko knew that his former colleagues at the Soviet Embassy would now have noticed his absence and the disappearance of the documents. He knew that the Soviet secret police, the NKVD, would be searching for him. No longer safe at home, he pleaded with a neighbour to let him and his family stay the night. During the night, four members of the NKVD broke into the Gouzenkos' apartment while Igor and Svetlana watched in terror through the neighbour's keyhole. The NKVD's forcible entry, watched by Mounties from this park, convinced the Canadian authorities that Gouzenko had an important story to tell.

On the morning of September 7, 1945, the RCMP escorted Gouzenko to the Department of Justice. His evidence persuaded the government of the existence of a major Soviet espionage campaign targeting the United States and Great Britain. Gouzenko and his family were taken into protective custody. Eventually, they were sequestered in a safe house at Camp X, a secret military training camp near Oshawa, Ontario.

On February 4, 1946, the Government of Canada appointed a Royal Commission headed by two Supreme Court Justices (the Taschereau-Kellock Commission) to look into Gouzenko's evidence. The Royal Commission's finding led the government of Prime Minister Mackenzie King to authorize the arrest and prosecution of twenty agents identified by the evidence, several working in government departments. Eleven were convicted and imprisoned, including a Member of Parliament.

The revelation that the USSR was spying against its allies stunned Canadians. A great sensation, the Gouzenko case was one of the first major international incidents in what became known as the 'Cold War'. Implicating major figures in the United States and Great Britain, it drew the attention of foreign governments and the international press.

The Gouzenkos were given a new identity in 1947. For the rest of his life, Gouzenko lived by an assumed name under which his family continues to live today. Despite the challenges of living under police protection in constant fear that the Soviets would track him down, Gouzenko lived a rewarding and creative life. When he died near Toronto in 1982, he knew that he had made the right choice.

"In our opinion, Gouzenko, by what he has done, has rendered a great public service to the people of this country and has thereby placed Canada in his debt."
Taschereau-Kellock Commission"

Following the ceremony, members of the Gouzenko family joined my family and friends for a dinner celebration at our home. The weather was good, so we sat in the garden and had a catered buffet meal with champagne. There were more speeches, toasts, hugs and celebration that lasted for several hours. It was exactly what I had dreamed of for years. I could not sleep that night as I reflected on the incredible day.

Post-Ceremony Media Coverage and Feedback

The ceremony was covered on the CBC and the CTV national news that evening. I saw Joy Malbon's CTV story several times the next morning on CTV NewsNet. The ticker on the bottom on the screen said "Ottawa honours daring Soviet defector as Hero". When I went by car, in the morning, to get the newspapers, I turned on the radio to the CBC. Evy's speech, recorded the previous day at the ceremony, was played as part of their "For the Record" secures. The speech sounded great. There were articles in the Ottawa newspapers. Steve Fisher, of CBC TV, subsequently informed me that his story played nationally on "Canada Now" national news program on June 4, at 6:00 p.m., and the next day on CBC Newsworld.

On Thursday I felt an incredible feeling of satisfaction and relief. Muscles that had been tense for years, finally relaxed and a heavy weight was off my shoulders. Evy Wilson arranged for me to get a replica of the plaque, which I proudly have on display at home.

On June 6, I spoke with Michel Audy, who told me that, in the eight years that he had been Executive Secretary of the HSMBC, no other file commemorating a person, place or event had received so much media attention. I received many messages of congratulations. It was all positive and fun. In the days that followed I sent letters of thanks to Mayor Chiarelli, Councillor Arnold, Tara Peel and Bernadine Clifford for their work on this project.

The Meaning and Consequences of the Commemorative Plaque

Notwithstanding the end of the Cold War, recent history, particularly the barbaric events of September 11, 2001, demonstrate that conflict is a constant in our world. Even though vast amounts of money are spent by western countries on intelligence gathering, the intelligence communities will never know everything. They will always benefit greatly from insiders in the enemies' camps coming forward and revealing what their enemies are up to. This plaque demonstrates that our society will always be grateful for such acts of courage.

The installation of the plaque was a partial payment for the moral debt owed by Canada and the Canadian people to this man who put in serious danger his wife, child and himself, in order to protect this country and its citizens and democratic system. What was particularly dangerous was that some citizens of this country, often as victims of naïve illusions about Soviet communism, committed themselves to offer their services as agents and spies. The documents delivered by Gouzenko to the Canadian government revealed the true nature of the Soviet policy and its sinister long-range planning to take over foreign countries from within.

Gouzenko's major concern was the intensity with which Soviet Intelligence pursued and penetrated American atomic energy research. He was aware that, God forbid, were the Soviets to build the bomb first, they would have no qualms in using it to destroy the Western powers and establish their rule worldwide. By supplying the Canadian authorities with his evidence, Gouzenko prevented further tragic developments to the cause of freedom everywhere. The transfer of Gouzenko's revelations, by Mackenzie King, to the President of the United States and the Prime Minister of the United Kingdom, forestalled and warded off much damage.

Gouzenko's story is more than one of courage. It is also about human integrity, clear judgment and a sense of responsibility. As a Russian-born person, raised and indoctrinated in the communist creed, he was nevertheless able to see and acknowledge the values on which Canada had been built and transcend tribal loyalties, to reveal the subversive intentions of his own government. For this the entire world owes him much. His act confirms the solidarity of all people of good will, regardless of their nationality, origin or creed. It was an impressive example of the triumph of the human individual, his personhood, his autonomy and capacity to overcome tribal instincts and indoctrination.

In erecting the plaque the City of Ottawa performed an historic event. The unveiling itself was a wonderful ceremony which generated much media coverage and raised the public's awareness of the Gouzenko Affair and its impact on Canadian and world history. The erection and unveiling of the plaque was a great event for the City of Ottawa, Canada and the Gouzenko family.

For the City of Ottawa and Canada the plaque served several purposes. It reminded us of our history and heritage and ensured that future generations and visitors to Dundonald Park will have an opportunity to learn of Igor Gouzenko's courage and contribution to the preservation of our freedom. The plaque also served to demonstrate a collective acknowledgment, as a society, of his heroic contribution to our lives. It serves as a reminder that individuals can achieve great things, and that such accomplishments are not just the stuff of stories from foreign lands, but that great historical events have also happened here. We have a history that is important, interesting, and inspiring. By unveiling the plaque in the formal way that it did, the City of Ottawa took a major step to ensure that it would not be forgotten.

For the Gouzenko family the plaque unveiling was particularly significant. According to Evy Wilson, the family has not had such consistent positive media coverage since the early 1950s. Alexandria Boire repeatedly told me, during the evening of June 4, that I had no idea what I had done for their family. She subsequently contacted me to say that a heavy veil had been lifted from her identity. For the first time she was feeling a particular kind of freedom that the rest of us take for granted.

The story of the plaque is an interesting case for sociological considerations. It reveals certain regularities in the functioning of bureaucracy, its tendency towards procrastination and inactivity. It shows how crucial it is that elected officials exercise their authority and not abdicate their responsibility to the bureaucratic machinery. I regret the lengthy process for the plaque to be unveiled and that Svetlana Gouzenko did not live to witness the ceremony. In the end, the institutions of bureaucracy behaved in a way consistent with their previous practice, including the behaviour they displayed when Igor Gouzenko escaped from the Soviet Embassy.

"All it takes for evil to triumph is for good people to do nothing." As long as there are people like Igor and Svetlana Gouzenko, tyranny has only limited potential.

CHAPTER 8: FUTURE CELEBRATIONS

While the unveiling of the City of Ottawa's commemorative plaque was a major step in honouring Igor Gouzenko, there may be several more in the future. Heritage Canada will unveil a commemorative bronze plaque in Dundonald Park in 2004. At the time of writing, Professor Martin Rudner, of the Norman Paterson School of International Relations at Carleton University is organizing a Gouzenko Symposium to discuss Gouzenko's impact on international intelligence and security during the Cold War, to be held on April 14-15, 2004, simultaneously with the federal plaque unveiling.

The Editorial, "Remember Gouzenko" which appeared in the June 4, 2003, *Ottawa Citizen*, suggested that a plaque was not enough to commemorate a man of Gouzenko's courage and that he deserved a star exhibit in the newly-announced Canada History Centre.[19]

---

[19] On May 26, 2003, Prime Minister Jean Chrétien announced the creation of a new museum in the nation's capital. The former Union Train Station, which has been a Government Conference Centre for years, will be converted into a new institution called the Canada History Centre. Its role will be to increase accessibility of all Canadians to their history and is expected to have travelling exhibitions to reach out to Canadians across the country. (Note: the government subsequently cancelled these plans.)

I subsequently learned that the National Archives and National Library will be responsible for the History Centre and contacted the appropriate officials to ensure that they were aware of the suggestion. The idea had an interesting spin-off. Just across from the Centre Block of the Parliament Buildings on Wellington Street is the old U.S. Embassy building, which will be open in a few years as the National Portrait Gallery. This Gallery will also be the responsibility of the National Archives. Accordingly, I contacted appropriate authorities and suggested that they should display at least two portraits of Gouzenko, one with his hood and one without. I hope they will also consider including a portrait of Svetlana Gouzenko.

In addition, the federal government is currently building a new War Museum in the capital, slated to open within a few years. There is a possibility that it may contain a section dedicated to the Cold War. I hope that a centerpiece exhibit will be about Igor Gouzenko.

Perhaps someday there will be an Igor and Svetlana Gouzenko Freedom Foundation which will preserve their names and forever continue on their behalf to contribute to our society, by supporting education and other initiatives that strengthen our democracy and civil liberties.

With time I hope that the name Igor Gouzenko will mean something special to more and more people and that visitors to Canada's capital will have an opportunity to learn about my hero's contribution to our collective history and freedom.

AFTERWORD

Before the City's plaque unveiling ceremony in April 2003 I contacted a number of people whom I thought might be interested in attending the event. One of them was Professor Martin Rudner at Carleton University who was a specialist in national security matters. He regretted that his schedule did not permit him to attend. However, I told him that there would be another occasion when the federal government unveiled its plaque the following year. He then proposed the idea of a conference at the same time as the unveiling ceremony. I told him that after four years of lobbying I was exhausted and had no energy to undertake the organizing of such an event. He appreciated my situation and suggested that he might organize a conference. I thought it was a great idea and hoped he would pursue it.

Professor Rudner and his colleagues ended up doing an outstanding job and organized a successful conference at Library and Archives Canada on April 14-15, 2019. The conference included speakers who were authorities on the Cold War and Soviet espionage, including Christopher Andrew, John F. Fox, Jr., Benjamin B. Fischer and Amy Knight. I was happy to have been given an opportunity to address the audience and discuss my efforts to commemorate Igor Gouzenko. In the morning of Thursday, April 15, Government officials unveiled the Historic Sites and Monument Board of Canada's plaque at a ceremony at the conference.

The drafting of the wording for the federal plaque was another step that demonstrated the necessity of constant and vigilant oversight of bureaucratic machinations. A few months prior I saw a first draft of the proposed plaque wording which made a reference to the wartime alliance with the Soviets without mentioning the Soviet record between 1939 and 1941. I wrote to the HSMBC to express my concern that their proposed wording may be interpreted as suggesting that the Soviets were allies from the beginning of the war. Fortunately, my objection was taken into account. The plaque wording is as follows:

"The Gouzenko Affair 1945-1946

The Gouzenko Affair brought the realities of the emerging Cold War to the attention of the Canadian public. On September 5, 1945, cipher clerk Igor Gouzenko left the Soviet Embassy with more than 100 documents which exposed the existence of a Soviet spy ring in Canada with links to others in the United States and Great Britain. His allegations gave rise to the creation in 1946 of a Royal Commission of Inquiry known as the Kellock-Taschereau Commission. Its confirmation of the country's vulnerability convinced the federal government to strengthen Canada's national security system."

While the conference continued that afternoon, the plaque was installed in Dundonald Park, next to the City of Ottawa plaque. After the conference, a number of participants went for a walk towards the park to see the two plaques. The sight of both of the plaques there almost took my breath away. It was a moment of sheer joy. A collection of papers delivered at the conference was subsequently published in 2006 as a book titled *"The Gouzenko Affair – Canada and the Beginnings of Cold War Counter-Espionage".*[20]

---

[20] J.L. Black and Martin Rudner (Eds.) *The Gouzenko Affair: Canada and the Beginnings of Cold War Counter-Espionage.* Newcastle: Penumbra Press, 2006.

Mission accomplished. It had been a long time since I had begun the lobbying process in 1999, and I was glad that it had come to such a successful conclusion.

The Gouzenko Affair continued to reverberate in the media over the years. Gordon Lunan wrote a book titled *"The Making of a Spy"* (1995) and then another one titled *"Redhanded"* before passing away in 2005 (published posthumously). David Shugar, one of the accused who was acquitted, emigrated to the country of his birth, Poland, and pursued an academic career. He passed away in 2015 at the age of 100.

The new Canadian War Museum opened in 2005. The entrance to the Cold War exhibit is dedicated to Igor Gouzenko and displays a huge image of him with his head covered. It graphically represents and symbolizes the giant that he was in that era.

Despite the end of the Cold War in 1991, Russian extraterritorial executions of those considered to be traitors have continued. In 2006 a former KGB and FSB officer who had been granted political asylum in the U.K., was murdered by poisoning (polonium). In 2018 a former Russian military intelligence officer (working for the same GRU organization that Gouzenko worked for) who was living in the U.K. was also poisoned (Novichok nerve agent) along with his daughter. They both survived. Clearly, more than 50 years since the death of Stalin, if Gouzenko were alive today, he would still be wise to take security precautions. Some things have come a long way over time, but others stay eerily the same.

Andrew Kavchak
October 2019

MISSION ACCOMPLISHED!

This picture was taken on April 15, 2004, in Dundonald Park, with the building at 511 Somerset Street West in the background. From left to right: Evelyn Wilson, Andrew Kavchak, Alexandria Boire. The federal plaque is on the left and the municipal plaque is on the right.

AN APPRECIATION

Throw me a sword, dear Lord, that I may slay the dragon.
For without the means to confront the beast, the challenge
is none, and the bravest gone.

We, Canada, owe Andrew Kavchak a sincere debt of gratitude. His skills and perseverance show us how to overcome overwhelming obstacles to achieve a worthy goal.

In December 2003, my dear sister Alex (Alexandria Boire), said it perfectly in her *Preface* to his book: *"Then Andrew Kavchak entered our life. Someone had contacted us who wanted to publicly honour the historic event and heroism of Igor and Sveltana Gouzenko!"*

His fateful phone call brought us together. Andrew understood. Through our respective families, we share a connection, a common bond of history forever forged by Soviet atrocities. I remain sincerely grateful that through his tireless efforts, our parents' sacrifices are recognized by Canada as an event of historic importance. I pray Andrew will continue to be successful in all of his endeavours.

Our parents were Soviet defectors Svetlana and Igor Gouzenko. We do not carry their surname. When they escaped from the USSR Embassy in Ottawa to warn the West of clandestine Soviet infiltration and perfidy, they did not expect to live. Miraculously, and by the grace of God, they survived to tell their story. The alarms were sounded. Canada was saved.

To this day, few understand the true story. The Soviets meant business. It was not 'spy vs spy' international espionage or James Bond theatrics. This was a full-scale *5th Column* invasion of democratic countries by a vile Soviet dictatorship with one purpose in mind: take-over from within.

Paranoia? No. They succeeded in many parts of the world. History is our proof. Our mother titled her unpublished memoirs *The Roman Goose*. It speaks of the fate of defectors to freedom from totalitarian regimes. The fable tells of Roman soldiers awakened by anxious geese who warned of an invading army. Then later in celebration, the Romans cooked these very same brave storm birds who sounded the alarm!

Even today, almost 75 years later, we are condemned by some for their actions to warn the West. *"One cannot be a traitor to tyranny"*, our parents protested, in defense.

Their story can *only* be told with a clear understanding of the grave reality faced then from the Soviet Union under Joseph Stalin.[21] Subsequently, through their proliferous networks and spy rings, Stalin's regime was about to develop its first atomic bomb! It was an unthinkable scenario. Our parents knew there would be no going back.

Decades later, following our dad's death in 1982, our mother had hoped for a Russia freed at last from the bonds of Soviet tyranny. Starting in 1989, her wish was realized with its sudden collapse. A new dawn promised long awaited changes within.

Eventually, the *'enemies of the people'* were exonerated, survivors and descendants repatriated. At last, in October 2017, the *Wall of Grief* was inaugurated in Moscow, a memorial dedicated to the victims of Stalin's repressions.[22] Sadly, this sentiment was short-lived and the nation is reverting once again to its former Soviet policies, at home and abroad.

---

[21] *He killed or imprisoned millions of his own people and lorded over one of the most repressive regimes in recent history. Sacrifices made by the Soviet people during Stalin's rule - the Gulag, the 'Great Terror', the mass repressions ... ",* Don Peleschuk, Global Post, March 2013.

[22] *"This terrifying past cannot be deleted from national memory. These actions cannot be justified by anything".* Today's Russian regime, the Kremlin, October 2017.

Set against these political realities, the story of Andrew's quest to honour our parents as Cold War heroes is a meticulous collection of first-hand recollections combined with key official exchanges taking place during a laborious process. We are in his shoes throughout this riveting tale.

Despite the inherent challenges, ultimately his book - like its subject matter - is a story of winning over seemingly impossible odds. He did it!

Thank you Andrew.

Evelyn Wilson
October 2019

CHRONOLOGY

January 26, 1919. Igor Gouzenko born in Russia.

June 1943. Gouzenko arrives in Canada.

September 1943. Svetlana Gouzenko arrives in Canada to join her husband in Ottawa.

May 8, 1945. Nazi Germany surrenders. Victory in Europe Day.

August 6, 1945. Atomic bomb is dropped on Hiroshima.

August 9, 1945. Atomic bomb is dropped on Nagasaki.

August 14/15, 1945. Initial announcement of Japan's surrender. Victory over Japan Day.

September 2, 1945. Japan formally surrenders in ceremony on *USS Missouri* in Tokyo Bay.

September 5-7, 1945. Gouzenko leaves the Soviet Embassy in Ottawa and defects.

February 5, 1946. After news of the Gouzenko defection was revealed on U.S. radio, the Canadian Cabinet appoints a Royal Commission of Inquiry.

June 27, 1946. Royal Commission issues its final report.

June 25, 1982. Igor Gouzenko passes away.

Summer 1999. Andrew Kavchak starts lobbying for the commemoration of the Gouzenko Affair.

July 28, 1999. First email to the Minister of Heritage Sheila Copps.

August 4, 1999. First email to Mayor of Ottawa Jim Watson.

January 14, 2000. HSMBC acknowledges receipt of the submission.

June 29, 2000. First contact with Gouzenko family and start of correspondence with Evelyn Wilson.

July 6, 2000. Mayor Watson announces his resignation.

July 20, 2000. Mayor Watson's letter to Svetlana Gouzenko confirms City of Ottawa plan unveil a plaque in the fall of 2000.

November 2000. City of Ottawa bureaucrats postpone plaque unveiling.

August 2001. City bureaucrats cancel plaque unveiling.

September 4, 2001. Svetlana Gouzenko passes away.

Fall 2001. Lobbying of City authorities to revive the application. City consults with federal Department of Foreign Affairs and International Trade (DFAIT).

June 6, 2002. City Clerk letter states that after consultations with DFAIT the City was cancelling the project.

July 19, 2002. Heritage Minister Sheila Copps makes official historic designation of the Gouzenko Affair as an event of national historic significance.

July 23, 2002. City Clerk indicates the matter will be reviewed.

September 5, 2002. Public Memorial Service held for Igor and Svetlana Gouzenko at cemetery in Mississauga, Ontario.

January 8, 2003. City authorities decide to proceed with plaque unveiling.

June 4, 2003. City plaque unveiling ceremony in Dundonald Park.

April 14-15, 2004. Conference held at Library and Archives Canada on the Gouzenko Affair.

April 15, 2004. HSMBC unveils the federal plaque at the conference and installs it in Dundonald Park next to the municipal plaque.

BIBLIOGRAPHY

Canada, 1946. Royal Commission to Investigate the Disclosure of Secret and Confidential Information to Unauthorized Persons (Final Report). Ottawa: Edmond Cloutier Printer.

J.L. Black and Martin Rudner (eds.). *The Gouzenko Affair, Canada and the Beginnings of Cold War Counter- Espionage*. Newcastle: Penumbra Press, 2006.

Robert Bothwell and J.L. Granatstein, (eds.). *The Gouzenko Transcripts*. Ottawa: Deneau Publishers & Company Ltd., 1982.

Callwood, June. *Emma, The True Story of Canada's Unlikely Spy*. Toronto: General Paperbacks, 1985.

Gouzenko, Igor. *This Was My Choice*. Toronto: J.M. Dent & Sons (Canada) Limited, 1948.

Gouzenko, Igor. *The Fall of a Titan*. London: Cassell & Company, Ltd., 1954.

Gouzenko, Svetlana. *Before Igor, My Memories of a Soviet Youth*. London: Cassell & Company Ltd., 1960.

Knight, Amy. *How the Cold War Began, The Gouzenko Affair and the Hunt for Soviet Spies*. Toronto: McClelland & Stewart Ltd., 2005.

Levy, David. *Fred Rose and Igor Gouzenko: The Cold War Begins*. Montreal: 2018.

Lunan, Gordon. *The Making of a Spy*, A Political Odyssey. Toronto: Robert Davies Publishing, 1995.

Sawatsky, John. *Gouzenko, The Untold Story*. Toronto: Macmillan of Canada, 1984.

Weisbord, Merrily. *The Strangest Dream, Canadian Communists, the Spy Trials, and the Cold War*. Toronto: Lester & Orpen Dennys Limited, 1983.

About the Author

Andrew Kavchak is a graduate of Concordia University (B.A.), Carleton University (M.A.), and Osgoode Hall Law School (LL.B.). He lives in Ottawa.

Made in the USA
Lexington, KY
24 October 2019